Glimpses of Fiddaman's Lynn

Life in Victorian King's Lynn seen through the eyes of James Fiddaman (1822-84)

Rosemary & Stan Rodliffe

First published in 2000 by Rodliffe Associates, 13 Chiltern Park, Thornbury, Bristol BS35 2HX

© Rosemary and Stan Rodliffe 2000

All Rights Reserved. No part of this publication may be reproduced, stored in a retrieval system, or transmitted in any form or by any means, electronic, mechanical, photocopying, recording or otherwise, without the prior permission of the publisher and copyright holders.

Typeset in Hoefler Text 11/16.5. Titles in Garamond Italic.

Originated by History into Print, The Local History Press Ltd,
3 Devonshire Promenade, Lenton, Nottingham. NG7 2DS.
Designed by Two Faces Design, 80 Watling Street, Towcester, Northants NN12 6BS
Printed by The Russell Press, Nottingham.

ISBN 0-9539356-0-4
British Library Cataloguing-in-Publication Data
A catalogue record for the book is available from the British Library.

Acknowledgements

We could not have written this book without the newspapers of the day, the *Lynn Advertiser* and *Lynn News*, which reported in such minute detail on the personalities, life and times of Victorian Lynn.

We are greatly indebted to the following people for helping with our research: the librarian and staff at King's Lynn Library; the curator and staff of King's Lynn Museums; the librarian and staff at Norfolk Studies Library, Norwich; Deirdre Sharp, archivist at the Library of the University of East Anglia; Andrew Lane and the Northend Trust at True's Yard Fishing Museum; Lynne Goodwin; Michael Hollway; Michael Langwade; Elizabeth Lloyd; Susan Overman; David Pitcher; Nanette Rawlinson; and volunteer researchers at Norfolk Family History Society. Our thanks to them all.

Contents

		Page number
1.	Introducing an uncommon tradesman	7
2.	Seeking fortune	9
3.	James Bowker	12
4.	'Derby day' at Lynn	15
5.	Settling at Lynn	22
6.	John Dyker Thew	25
7.	Fiddaman's hotel	29
8.	John J. Lowe	36
9.	Sporting house	39
10.	Civic celebrations	45
11.	Francis Joseph Cresswell	52
12.	Form, Form, Riflemen Form!	56
13.	Lynn Races revived	64
14.	Superintendent George Ware & the Borough Police	73
15.	Lynn Regatta	84
16.	Lynn Gala	93
17.	Frederick Fiddaman	101
18.	Frederick Savage	103
19.	Alfred Dodman	107
20.	Agricultural shows	110
21.	Wine and spirit merchants	115
22.	Summer parties	120
23.	Captain John Hillman Howard & the *Spindrift*	125
24.	Never quite a gentleman?	132
25.	The legacy	138
Chronology of significant events		140
Mayors of Lynn		144

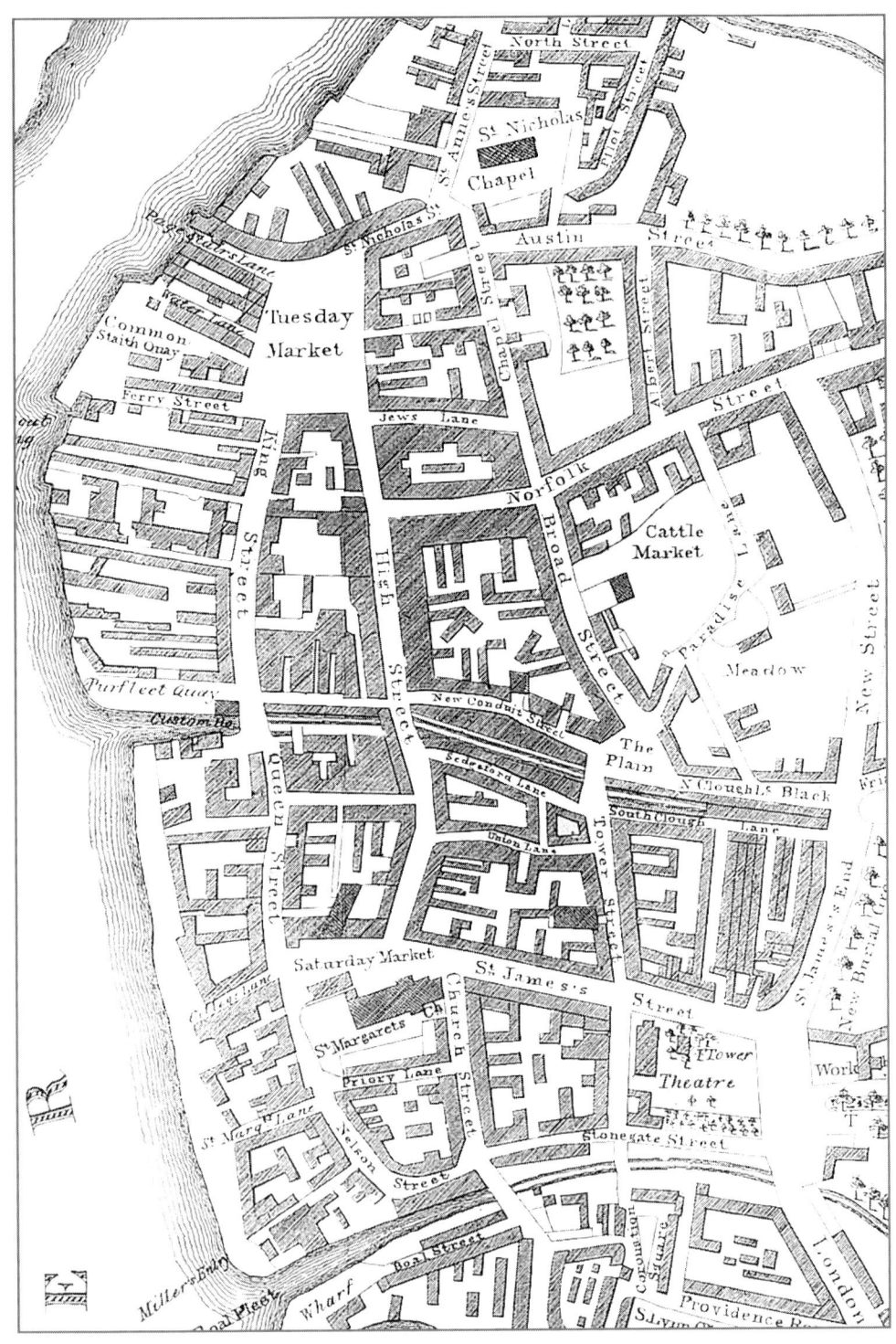

Detail from a plan of King's Lynn published by Longbottom in 'Handbook of King's Lynn or a visit to the Metropolis of Marshland' compiled by W.P. Burnet, London 1846

Reproduced by kind permission of the Library of the University of East Anglia

In Memory *of*
Tom & Vera Blomfield

Fiddaman and Lowe in the Corn Exchange on 1 April 1869 preparing to serve dinner to the Lynn Loyal & Constitutional Association. The occasion celebrated the defeat of a petition against the election of Robert Bourke.

Photograph courtesy of National Monuments Record Centre; copyright Phillips

Chapter 1

Introducing an uncommon tradesman

Grandfather Thomas Fiddaman Blomfield (1883-1953) was a butcher at King's Lynn. For a long time his middle name was a puzzle. We found no Fiddaman amongst his ancestors. We had heard of Fiddaman's Hotel in Norfolk Street because it was very conveniently placed for the cattle market where father, Tom Blomfield (1906-62), would take a lunch-time drink with his friends each market Tuesday after buying cattle for slaughter or grading livestock. But why would grandfather have been named after a publican? And who was Fiddaman?

An obituary in the *Norfolk Chronicle* in January 1884 raised even more questions:

> Died, at Kings Lynn, Mr James Fiddaman. He began life in very humble circumstances and without the advantages offered by education. The son of a tailor in a small way of business, he first acted as assistant to his uncle, who was ostler at a tavern in Lynn. He was afterwards ostler or "boots" at inns and hotels in neighbouring towns, subsequently he tramped the country for a time, visiting London, Brighton, and other places in quest of a good situation. Eventually he returned to Lynn, took a public-house known as the Wheatsheaf, in Norfolk Street, and made it the local centre of the sporting interest in West Norfolk. After a time he bought the house, converted it into an hotel and wine vaults, and rapidly made a fortune. Mr Fiddaman was a munificent donor to many benevolent institutions, and his private acts of charity were numerous. An enormous concourse of persons attended his funeral.

How had James risen from life on the tramp to become such a popular and wealthy man? His estate was valued at over £8,000; at least £350,000 in today's money. This was at a time when a labourer might earn 20s (£1) for a six day week of ten hour days. Bricklayers, carpenters, and smiths commanded 30s a week; engineers earned 50s. Rent for a house in Pleasant row or Begley's buildings cost between £6 and £8 per year. The poorest lived in the yards, such as Atto's, where weekly rents were 1s 8d for a single room, 2s 6d if furnished, and 2s 2d for a two roomed cottage.

We still cannot decide whether James was ever accepted as a 'gentleman', a title, which according to the *Encyclopaedia Britannica* of 1845 was by courtesy 'generally accorded to all persons above the rank of common tradesman when their manners are indicative of a certain amount of refinement and intelligence'. Whatever else he might have been, he was certainly no 'common tradesman'!

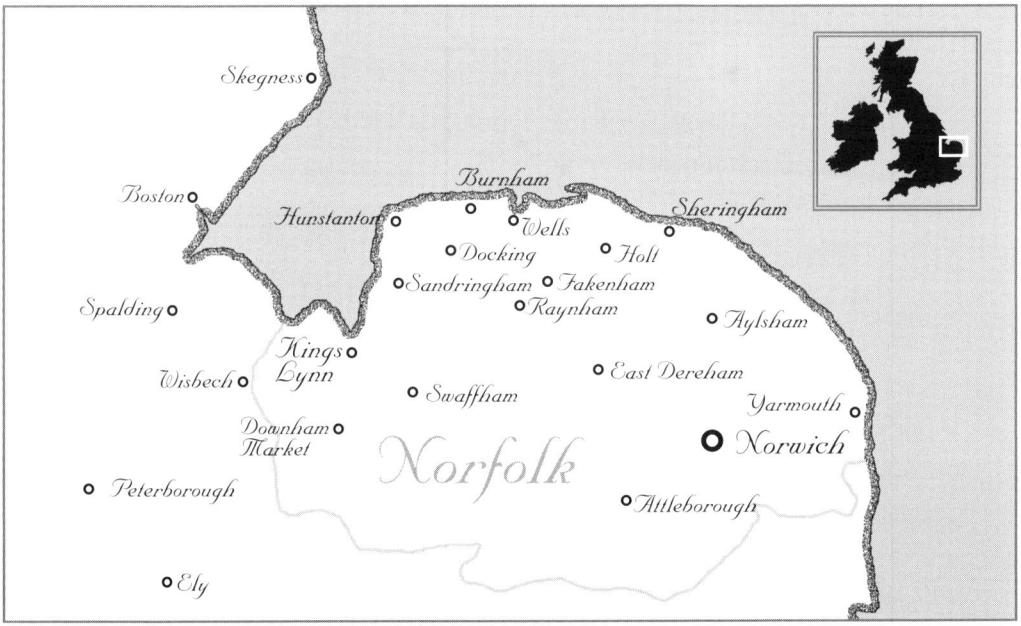

County of Norfolk

Chapter 2

Seeking fortune

Out of Fakenham

The small town of Fakenham lies in the county of Norfolk on the north bank of the river Wensum, about one hundred miles north of London, 22 miles east of King's Lynn, and 25 miles north west of Norwich. By the early nineteenth century, it was a thriving market town of 1,500 or so inhabitants whose prosperity depended on the surrounding great estates of Holkham, Houghton and Raynham, where the agricultural revolution had been born. Its market was held every Thursday and, although it handled some cattle, sheep and pigs, its major business was the sale of corn. Large numbers of millers, maltsters and merchants would come from Wells, Blakeney and Brancaster to buy grain from the farmers who carried their samples in small leather cases. It had annual fairs on Ash Wednesday and 11 November and was renowned for extensive shows of cattle on the heath in Hempton parish south of the river on Whit Tuesday and 22 November.

James Fidget Fiddaman was the eldest child of Thomas Fiddaman and Ann, born at Fakenham on 7 April 1822. Twelve days later he was baptised in St Peter's church. He had seven brothers and sisters, all born at Fakenham except Francis Fidget who was born at Wells in 1832. Sister Fanny, born in 1824, became servant to Robert Barnes the school master at Church Close Academy, Burnham Westgate; she had a daughter Susan. Youngest sister Ann, born in 1843, married George Flegg and lived in London, working as a housekeeper, until she was widowed in her late thirties when she took her young family to live in the city of Oxford.

Brother Francis married Charlotte Cape in the 1850s and set up home at nearby Hempton, where he worked as a porter and delivery van driver for the railway company. His only son, Frederick Fidget, was born in late October 1858 but tragically died before Christmas. His daughter Maud was only six years old when she died after a short illness in 1882. His daughter Fannie married Albert Robinson of Great Grimsby, Lincolnshire, and was the only next of kin when he died intestate in 1889, leaving little to show for his ventures as a fishmonger, fish merchant and keeper of a beer house. James' father was a labourer and a higgler, an itinerant dealer, but he was remembered variously as 'a fish dealer who travelled the country' and as 'a tailor in a small way of business'. No doubt there was an element of truth in both descriptions since a higgler would buy at one place and sell at another, dealing in anything which offered an opportunity to earn a living. Perhaps James glamorised his childhood, the travels with his father to the towns and villages around Fakenham, the years in which he began to develop his entrepreneurial skills

On the tramp

James left home in his late teens, having had no formal education, except for Sunday-school. He went to assist his uncle James who was ostler for Richard Garman at the Three Tuns inn, Church street, King's Lynn. It was here that he forged his lifelong friendship with John J. Lowe, who would become his partner in many business ventures. He was quick to learn about horses and the work of the stable. He soon moved to the Queens Head inn, at Downham, which was kept by a brother of Richard Garman, where he was a 'boots', a general servant amongst whose duties was cleaning guests' boots. He left this job some time before 1845 to seek his fortune further afield, visiting London, Brighton and Hastings. The railway to London had yet to be built. His fare on the stage coach, even travelling as an 'outsider', was more than his wages for a week. So he travelled on foot. Going 'on the tramp' was the accepted way of avoiding a local slump and improving prospects of employment.

On his travels he occasionally had to endure severe hardships. He was reasonably comfortable while he was working as an ostler or 'boots', particularly when he had gained a position at one of the better hotels. Otherwise he was vulnerable to the squalid conditions and dubious companionship of life in low lodging houses and was subjected to the temptations of begging, or worse, to survive.

He returned to Lynn, much wiser but no richer, and began work for Henry Garner at the Rummer inn, Tower street. Once again he moved on: to Wisbech, to the Rose and Crown and afterwards the White Hart; and then the Crown hotel, Swaffham, a posting inn kept by William Page. He finally returned to Lynn around 1849 to work as an ostler at the Star inn, 13 Norfolk street, where the landlord was Henry Wanty. It was around this time that James met two more lifelong friends. One was James Bowker, a well-educated young man from a Lynn merchant family. The other was John Overman.

John Overman

John was born at Burnham on 21 May 1816 into a family which had for generations been tenant farmers under Lord Leicester. His grandfather, Robert John Overman (1752-1808), had introduced Southdown sheep into Norfolk from Sussex. His father, John Robert Overman (1791-1853), farmed almost one thousand acres in the vicinity of Burnham Sutton and at South Creake and was highly regarded by H.W. Keary, the Holkham Agent. His elder brother, Robert Wright Overman (1815-74), took over the tenancy of nearby Egmere farm in his own right in 1852 while John took over the Burnham farms when his father died. John was renowned for his fat cattle which took many prizes at both Norwich and Smithfield shows. His cattle and crossbred sheep often featured on the Christmas stalls of the Burnham butchers; in 1869 one of his small Brittany bullocks, weighing about 60 stone, was acclaimed as a model specimen of the 'marbled beef of Old England'.

It was John's interest in sport which triggered his friendship with James Fiddaman. Coursing was one of his great passions and in 1858 his black bitch, *Victoria*, was particularly successful in the Burnham Cup Stakes. The meeting that year spread over several days and, on the first and third, was hosted by John on his farm at Burnham Sutton.

John died on the morning of Monday 14 November 1887. Four days later his coffin was borne to Burnham Westgate churchyard by twelve estate workers, accompanied by four hundred mourners. They were led by members of the Sussex Farm Lodge of Oddfellows, each of whom paid their last respects by dropping a spray of lemon thyme into the grave.

Chapter 3

James Bowker

Merchant heritage

James was born at Lynn in 1828, the youngest of Alexander and Elizabeth Bowker's three children. The family had lived in St Margaret's Place and run their business from an office at this same address for several generations, certainly since 1776, when an earlier Alexander Bowker had been a corn, coal and seed merchant.

James Bowker, Mayor of Lynn 1883 and '84
Photograph courtesy of the Borough Council of King's Lynn and West Norfolk

During James' boyhood the family lived in Germany and Italy, partly for the benefit of his father's health and partly because his father was concerned that the children should receive a good education. James was educated mainly at Pisa and it was here that he gained the mastery over European languages for which he was to be renowned in later life. He went to sea as a young man, serving as a purser on South African mail steamers operated by the Royal Mail Steamship Company, before returning to Lynn and setting up James Bowker & Co as a ship-broker. His friendship with James Fiddaman began around this time when, as young men from very different backgrounds, they both struggled to make their mark. James' father had retired by 1850 and the affairs of the family business, then known as A. & J. Bowker, were managed by James and his brother Alexander until 1870 when his brother died leaving James in sole charge.

On 25 April 1862 at St Margaret's church, James married Marion Stafford Eyre, youngest daughter of Elijah Eyre, the well-known brewer. He became a partner in Elijah Eyre & Co when his father-in-law died. By the 1880s he had built a wide range of business interests: steamship owner; Lloyds agent for the port of Lynn; agent for the Rock Life and Scottish Imperial Fire Offices; and managing partner of West Norfolk Coal Company. For many years he was vice-consul for Italy and Austria.

Prominent Tory

James' involvement in the social and municipal life of Lynn did not blossom until nearly twenty years after the marriage of his sister Emma to Lewis Whincop Jarvis in 1852. He became active in Tory politics in the late 1860s and was a regular speaker at meetings of the Lynn Loyal and Constitutional Association where J. Dyker Thew recalled that 'the feast of reason and the flow of beer used to occupy the principal part of the evening'.

He was returned to represent the North Ward in the Town Council along with J.K. Jarvis in 1872 when they defeated W. Clark and D.C. Burlingham. He was subsequently returned unopposed on four occasions so that he was a Town Councillor for fifteen consecutive years. He was held in the highest esteem by his political opponents. He was a JP for the borough and a Municipal Charity Trustee. He was elected Mayor of the borough in November 1883 and carried out his duties so satisfactorily that he was unanimously re-elected to serve a further year. Two tragedies struck during his mayoralties. His wife died on 14 September 1884 and he personally suffered a stroke during the following March from which he never fully recovered.

Invalid for the rest of his life

His stroke occurred in most dramatic circumstances. As Mayor, he was the presiding magistrate at the trial of Robert Brooks, a man who was notorious for his violent behaviour. On this occasion James was so extremely agitated by Brooks that he was struck down by paralysis while the court was still sitting and had to be carried home.

Thereafter James took little part in public affairs although he was elected an alderman in November 1886 and served for six years. He continued to run A. & J. Bowker, now in partnership with his nephew, Mr F.W. Jarvis, one of the four sons of Sir Lewis Whincop Jarvis and Emma. He married for a second time on 20 July 1887 at Yarmouth to Mary Sophia Moyse, a daughter of Walter Moyse, several times Mayor of Lynn. In 1891 he transferred A. & J. Bowker to Mr R.O. Ridley and retired to Southsea. He had a lifelong passion for travel which he was still able to indulge in his last years, visiting Egypt and Madeira as well as many European resorts.

James died at Southsea on Monday 1 September 1902. On the following Friday afternoon his body arrived by rail at Lynn, lying in a splendid polished oak coffin with brass fittings, accompanied by his widow. His body was laid to rest at Hardwick road cemetery alongside that of his first wife, Marion Stafford.

Chapter 4

'Derby Day' at Lynn

Horse racing, gambling, crime and deception

It would be surprising, given James Fiddaman's background, if he had not taken a keen interest in horse racing in general and the first Lynn Races in particular. And since horse racing and gambling were inseparable, it is natural to wonder whether his change of fortune might have been associated in some way with Lynn Races.

Horse racing was riddled with crime and deception in the early years of Victoria's reign. It was not uncommon for a jockey, trainer or stable lad to take a bribe to nobble his horse or to encourage longer odds by spreading stories. The turning point was reached when the 1844 Derby was won by a quite well-known four-year-old horse called *Maccabeus*, masquerading as three-year-old *Running Rein*. Lord George Bentinck, MP for Lynn from 1828 until his death in 1848, played a key role in the exposure of this fraud. By the time of the first Lynn Races in 1850, fortunes were still won and lost on the racecourse but many dishonest practices had been stamped out thanks to the efforts of Lord George Bentinck amongst others.

Bollin's brainchild

Lynn Races were most probably the brainchild of Robert Henry Bollin, keeper of the Duke's Head on Tuesday Market place. That was certainly the view of Walter Moyse, the Mayor, at the banquet in the Duke's Head after the event. But Bollin, well-rewarded by the pleasures of providing a hearty meal and fine wine to a large gathering, generously insisted that Walter Moyse should take the credit.

The course was on 50 acres of pasture at West Lynn, just over the Free Bridge on the way to Clenchwarton. The land was rented by two farmers, Thomas Mawby and James Baker, who made it available despite the threat of fines and penalties from their landlords, the Eau Brink Commissioners. The organising committee offered to make good any damage and began preparing the land, which had been the river bed before the Ouse was straightened by the Eau

Brink Cut. Frederic Cruso, civil engineer and son of Robinson Cruso, Lynn's postmaster at the time, oversaw the filling of creeks and levelling, giving his services free of charge. The work took nearly a month and cost almost £100. The result was a course, about a mile round, with curves at each end which were considered 'a little too sharp'. Jockeys rated it 'equal to any other course in the kingdom - those of one or two towns excepted'. A substantial grandstand was built on the north side of the field.

Local lovers of the sport had subscribed over £150 towards the stakes and there were six races on the card. Entries had to be made at the Duke's Head hotel on or before Monday 9 September. There would be no race unless three horses started. The correct cards showing more than sufficient riders and runners for all six events came out on the Tuesday. *The Lynn Advertiser* congratulated the committee on organising 'a good day's out-door amusement' for 'our holiday-making and race-going townsfolk'.

First Lynn Race Day

The great day arrived: Wednesday 11 September 1850. Cloud partially obscured the sun but the conditions were reasonable for racing and spectators. The event had been advertised widely; the East Anglian and Eastern Counties Railways ran special trains. The first race was due to start at 12 o'clock. Walter Moyse, Robert Bollin and the other members of the committee, amongst whom were John Platten and R. Braithwaite, must have been wondering whether their hard work would be rewarded. They need not have worried. The sight was spectacular: 'Derby day' at Lynn. A crowd of 20,000 to 30,000 had gathered. The morning trains had brought nearly 5,000; the remainder poured in from Lynn and its surroundings. The gentry and the well-to-do filled the grandstand from where they had a full view of the course. There were about twenty refreshment booths at the east end of the field. Along the south side, waggons and carts were drawn up for those who wished to pay for the better view provided by a 'higher standing'. A half mile line of carriages, horses unattached, was drawn up in the centre of the ground and packed with spectators. Beyond these were gigs and pony carts. Admission to the ground was: 2s 6d for four-wheeled carriages drawn by two horses, 1s 6d if drawn by one; 1s for gigs; and 6d for horses. Thousands of spectators on foot crowded against the cords which bounded the course. There were amusements: tight rope dancers, acrobats, Ethiopian serenaders and more.

It was, reported the *Lynn Advertiser,* 'a motley crowd - in goodly motley, for all were dressed in their best - and you saw they had made up their minds to be happy'.

The police were present in considerable strength: the rural force under Superintendent George Ogden; and the borough force under Superintendent Thornton. They were to protect racegoers from three-card tricksters, magsmen (pitch-and-toss operators) and other cheats, who plagued race meetings at the time. Their efforts were apparently well-rewarded because the magistrates were presented with a clean sheet on the following day.

Walter Moyse, Francis Hulton - a local timber merchant - and Stephen Abbott, a farmer of 1,200 acres at Wicken Farm, officiated as stewards; Mr J. Clarke of Newmarket was the judge; Robert Bollin acted as clerk of the course, assisted by the members of the race committee and other gentlemen. Bollin must have found his job quite stressful because he later admitted to 'hasty expressions' which he hoped would be excused. Was some of his stress caused by the absence of a starter? It is not clear whether this key position had been overlooked by the committee or whether the incumbent had panicked and withdrawn at the thought of performing this tricky and thankless task in the presence of such a large crowd. Either way, in stepped John Gamble, a Shouldham farmer, who accepted the duty 'on the spur of the moment' and performed it to the satisfaction of all concerned.

The novelty of the day generated great excitement. The riders were weighed. The bell rang announcing that horses were about to be saddled in front of the grandstand. People on horseback, closely followed by those on foot, converged from all over the ground. Here were the riders in their owner's colours: apricot and purple cap; blue and white; blue body, scarlet sleeves and black cap; black and yellow stripe; pink and black cap; yellow and scarlet cap. If anyone had been thinking of placing a bet, now was the last chance to study the form. Mr Rayner's *Pulcherrima*, a four year old ridden by Rogers, took first places in both heats of the first race, the West Norfolk Stakes, to become the first ever winner at Lynn Races. The other five races went off successfully and the card was completed by six o'clock. The journey home provided its own spectacle, a continuous stream of vehicles from the Eau Brink Bridge to Lynn, reported in the *Lynn Advertiser:*

As we slowly wended our way amongst the pedestrians, we were passed by elegant private carriages, hackney coaches, omnibuses with overflowing loads inside and out, dog carts, buggies, sociables, gigs, &c., &c., horses of all sorts, sizes, colors, and breeds; one eyed, no eyed, wind-galls, spavins, and roarers, forming altogether such a strange diversity of characters, of costumes, of expressions, of manners, and appearance as created to the observant spectator, a scene of unparalleled amusement and interest. It was indeed surprising that no damage was done to life and limb, when it was considered how many thousands of persons of all descriptions were huddled in so small a space, but all was marked by that good humour, order, and regularity, so characteristic of Englishmen.

Celebrations in the town

The success of the first Lynn Races was celebrated that night with a banquet, the stewards' ordinary, at the Duke's Head hotel in a room tastefully decorated with flags and evergreens. More than sixty gentlemen - stewards, patrons, owners and their guests - sat down to an evening of feasting, entertainment and toasting organised by the host, and instigator of the Races, Robert Bollin. The Mayor, Walter Moyse, was in the chair; Frederic Cruso and John Gamble were the vice chairs. The spread was lavish: soups of mock turtle, gravy and vermicelli; entrées of turbot, fried soles and stewed eels; roast beef, boiled beef, fillet of veal, lamb, haunch of mutton, ham, tongue, chickens, ducks, geese, calf's head, pigeon pies, veal, game and lobsters; topped off with trifle, tipsey cake, jellies, blancmange, syllabubs, custards, rice-puddings, lemon-puddings, cheese cakes, plum tarts and apple.

Once they had eaten their fill, the tables were cleared. Wines and an excellent dessert were placed on the table. The Mayor stood to propose the health of Her Majesty the Queen, His Royal Highness Prince Albert, the Royal Family. Unexpectedly, Frederic Cruso intervened to propose the Army and the Navy, coupled with the health of Captain Grounds. The Mayor swiftly recovered his composure, proposing another dozen toasts, some with musical honours. Every toast was celebrated with loud cheers and enthusiastic supping. At carefully chosen intervals, Mr Smirke provided respite with songs such as: 'Woman loves ye best', 'Beautiful Venice', and 'The Lass O'Gowrie'. Everyone shared Frederic Cruso's hopes that the races might be permanently established and the Mayor gave a final toast 'Our next merry meeting in 1851'. It was eleven o'clock when the gentlemen left for home.

That night the Crown Gardens and Tuesday Market were packed with revellers enjoying fireworks and other amusements to mark the end of the first Lynn Race Day. Was James Fiddaman amongst them celebrating? His luck had certainly changed by March the following year because he was neither ostler nor 'boots' but was portraying himself as a gentleman, born at Raynham rather than Fakenham!

Oil skin, mackintosh and umbrella!

Encouraged by their success, the organisers extended Lynn Races to two days in August 1851. Subscribers made nearly £250 available for prize money, there was a full card of five races each day, and the Great Northern Railway ran cheap trains. But the weather was tempestuous; the crowds stayed away. The following year, undeterred, the organisers redoubled their efforts and generous subscribers almost doubled the prize money. Once again two days in August were chosen. The *Lynn Advertiser* captured the scene on Wednesday 11 August 1852 as racegoers struggled to the course:

> Rain, rain, rain, wind, wind, splash, dash, oil skin, mackintosh, and umbrella! But what matter? We are bent on a day's enjoyment, and that we will have, come what may. What if the omnibuses do set us down on the outer verge of a kind of Slough of Despond Redivivus, through which we must wade ancle-deep, aye, much more than ancle-deep, to arrive at the ground. What if our garments are soaked, and our faces daubed with mud thrown up by carriage wheels and horses hoofs? "It will all rub off when its dry;" and so in the best of spirits, after, perchance, assisting a fair friend over a miry field or two and up and down a slippery pair of steps, we remove some of the superfluous mud adhering to our boots, in a friendly heap of straw, and turn our attention to the attractions of the race-course, by which we are now standing.

The attractions included side shows and refreshments but, no matter which way spectators might turn, they were confronted by the sellers of 'correct cards', whose attentions that year were recorded for posterity by the *Lynn Advertiser*:

> We have not advanced many steps 'ere our ears are assailed with an announcement of the never-to-be-forgotten 'true and correct card of the races, with the names, weight and colours of the riders,' screamed forth in shrill accents by a sun-burnt gipsy-looking woman. At the next step a little boy obtrudes the same very essential cards on our notice; and then a husky man of nondescript profession brandishes his stock of cards in our face, roaring the same announcement in our ears. At length we find that the only means of relieving ourselves from their importunities is to purchase a card, and carry it about in our hands.

Only 3,000 braved the elements to enjoy that day at the races. The booths did little trade; neither the sparring booth, nor the sellers of oysters, apples and meat pies, nor even George Laws, the wine and spirit merchant from High street Lynn who had set out his store of fine wines and refreshments beneath the shelter of the grandstand. The weather improved overnight and throughout the second day, eventually attracting 10,000 or so to the course.

Left in the dark

The organisers took stock of their disappointments and decided not to hold the event in 1853. The following year saw their final attempt to establish Lynn Races. Robert Bollin, assisted by Richard Whitwell, a local veterinary surgeon, managed to raise subscriptions totalling nearly £100 and one day's racing was arranged for 4 October. The day came, the weather was splendid, and the going was good but the crowds were slow to arrive and numbered only a few thousand by four o'clock. The first heat of the West Norfolk Stakes over a mile and a quarter was started at half past twelve, half an hour late, which proved to be a delay with serious consequences. Mr Hinde's five year old bay mare *Miss Goldsmidt* was the winner in an exciting contest with a close finish, going on to win the second heat similarly and walking over in the third. The Lynn Handicap, Stewards' Plate, and Open Hurdle Race followed smoothly and provided some thrilling moments. It was then that the consequence of the promised twenty minute interval between heats began to be noticed. The Hunters' Stakes, over one mile and four flights of hurdles, did not start until about six o'clock. By then it was so dark that the colours of the jockeys were indistinguishable from the stand and most of the spectators had given up and gone home! At the Duke's Head that night, Robert Bollin consoled himself with the profits from the Stewards' Ordinary, tickets 3s 6d each, but for him Lynn Races were history.

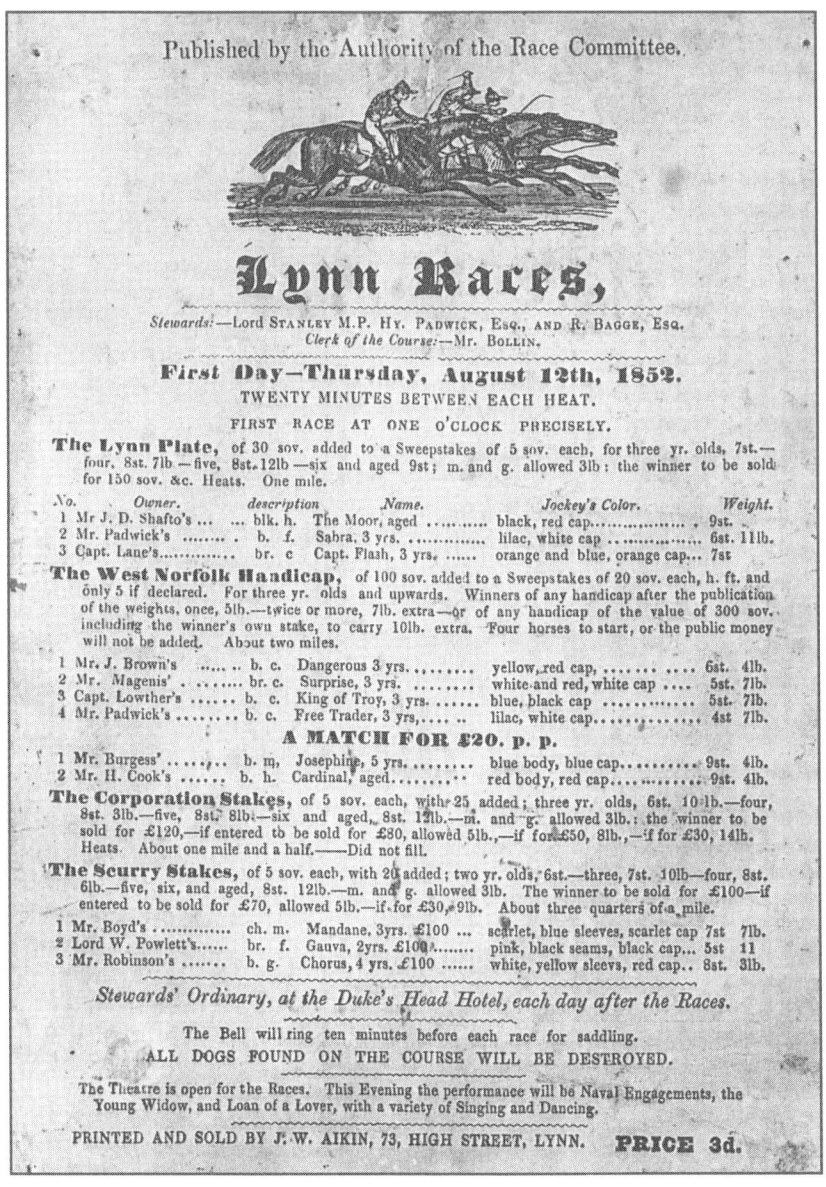

A 'correct card' from Lynn Races 1852
Courtesy of King's Lynn Museums

Chapter 5

Settling at Lynn

Dreaming

James Fiddaman's imagination had been fired by the excitement surrounding 'Derby Day' at Lynn in 1850. With an annual meeting and rapidly expanding railways bringing increasing crowds, he could see Lynn quickly becoming a sporting mecca in West Norfolk. He had relished the atmosphere at the Duke's Head, where Robert Bollin had masterminded the races, and he began to dream of his own hotel where gentlemen could meet in comfortable surroundings to discuss form and discreetly place a wager. Towards the end of March 1851 James was in Lynn investigating the possibilities. He stayed at 24 Chapel street with Matthew Feaks, a coachman whose ambition was to be an innkeeper.

Lynn Harbour
Photograph courtesy of National Monuments Record Centre; copyright Phillips

Town and trade

Lynn was outwardly prosperous with a population of twenty thousand depending on the wealth generated by its port and farming in West Norfolk. The port was the trade gateway to the world for six counties served by the river Ouse and its tributaries. Ten years before, as a lad at the Three Tuns inn, James had spent many hours on the quayside watching the porters at work. Unloading ships carrying timber from the Baltic and America, coal from Durham and Northumberland, corn from northern Europe, oil cake from Holland and wine from Spain and Portugal. Loading produce for London and white sand for glass making at Newcastle and Leith. Transferring goods to and from the horse drawn lighters for the trade inland. James admired the acumen of the merchants who had made their fortunes from these cargoes but sometimes wondered who counted the cost of those lives lost in shipwrecks far from home. He hoped to find a site for his hotel sufficiently far from the river to discourage quayside porters, cosmopolitan sailors and the army of navvies who were excavating the Estuary cut.

James enjoyed the bustle and hubbub of Tuesdays and Saturdays at Lynn as the narrow streets filled with scores of carriers' carts, farmers' waggons and shoppers drawn to the thriving markets from as far as twenty miles away. On Tuesdays, the streets were even more congested as thousands of cattle were driven through to and from the livestock market on Paradise field, bringing farmyard fragrance and decoration to the town. At the end of a long day at the markets or Corn Exchange, many of the farmers would retire to an inn for food, drink and sport before making their way unsteadily homewards. James had seen many of them enjoying shooting matches and coursing events. His hotel would need to be nearby the markets if he was to win their custom.

Farmers, gentry and their families flocked to Lynn for the shopping, particularly for the latest fashions. Of the hundred or so shops in High street, over forty were for clothing: drapers; tailors and outfitters; hatters and milliners; furriers, glovers, haberdashers and hosiers; boot makers, shoemakers and a stay manufacturer. Many of these shopkeepers were quite wealthy, as were the tradesmen who supplied them, and James hoped to attract them to his hotel, especially those who had shown such a keen interest in Lynn Races.

Norfolk Street

There were several well-established hotels in the town, most relying heavily on commercial travellers for their trade. James liked the style of the Tuesday Market place and would have jumped at an opportunity to run either the Dukes Head or the Globe but both were well beyond his pocket. Norfolk street lay midway between the Tuesday Market place and Paradise field. It was more affordable and the area from High street to the junction with Chapel and Broad streets escaped the worst of the offensive stenches and fevers of the yards.

The yards of Lynn were home to one third of the population. They had been the gardens and courtyards of the fine properties lining the main streets until the booming population encouraged their development for housing. Impressive façades hid notoriously insanitary and overcrowded conditions. It was not uncommon for as many as twenty houses to be served by a single tap or pump. Their communal privies were always foul, often full up to the seats, and box privies were frequently emptied unlawfully into the street. In the worst, litter, excrement and refuse lay in heaps; drains were blocked with abominable accumulations of dung and filth. Diseases such as cholera, smallpox and influenza took a heavy toll.

There were several suitable properties in Norfolk street, including the Star inn, at the junction with Broad street, where only a year ago James had been working as an ostler. Henry Wanty ran it as a lodging house, filling it with labourers working on the Estuary cut. The nearest hotel was the Black Horse in Chapel street, where Thomas and Ann Springall catered for commercial travellers from all over Europe. The Star or the Black Horse would be ideal for James' purposes if either should come on the market.

Jemima

James made his plans. He knew that he could count on help from several old friends. John J. Lowe, born and bred at Lynn and now a master baker, would advise him on suppliers of victuals. James Bowker and John Overman would introduce him to the sporting fraternity of town and country. And now he had met Jemima Carse, an attractive girl in her twenties, born at Lynn, the daughter of Hugh and Elizabeth. She was a barmaid at the Black Horse and James had decided to ask her if she would share his dream. He began reading the *Lynn Advertiser* most carefully each week.

Chapter 6

John Dyker Thew

Born to the Lynn Advertiser

John Dyker Thew was born on 2 November 1824, the only son of John Thew, founder of the *Lynn Advertiser*; his sister, Fanny, was born the next year. Educated at Lynn Grammar School, under the Rev John Bransby, he spent many hours avidly reading books from the Subscription Library, developing a lasting interest in literature and periodicals. In later life he admitted that the library had had another attraction when, in the evening, it became 'the happy hunting ground of all the town gossips'. His father put him to work in his printing business at an early age, ensuring that he served his apprenticeship in every department. He eventually became a partner with his father and joint proprietor of the paper. Over a period of more than fifty years, he helped to build the newspaper from a small local advertising circular into an influential publication which reported, with unfailing accuracy and good humour, on the personalities, life and times of Victorian Lynn.

He did not keep a diary but in 1890 he wrote a series of 'Personal Recollections; by a Lynn Sexagenarian' for the columns of the *Lynn Advertiser*. Published as a book shortly before his death, the reminiscences are a fascinating insight into the affairs of the town and the lives of its public men.

Family man

On 14 July 1848, John Dyker married Jane, the daughter of William Smith Simpson, a contractor from Ely who had made his fortune constructing railways, including that from Lynn to Downham. They were blessed with seven sons and five daughters. Three of the sons died before their father: William Henry; Percy; and John Dyker Jr, who drowned off Prawle Point in South Devon. Four sons prospered: Herbert became an accomplished organist; Walter worked for the London and Provincial Bank; Frederick Sherwood was ordained after reading theology at Cavendish College; and Frank Simpson became the junior partner in the family business. Gertrude died in childhood but the other daughters married well: Jane Elizabeth to George Howlett of Melbourne, Australia; Fanny to Clement Edward Priestley, a GP; Florence Gertrude to Edward William Betts of Babingley; and Helen Eliza to Colonel Thomas Millard Bento Eden.

St Ann's House, in St Ann's street, was the family home for many years. A fine old mansion with a handsome stone front, according to tradition, it had been a town house of the Walpole family. Until the middle of the 19th century it had been occupied by the Allen family, whose country residence was Shouldham Hall. Its staircase was splendid, with leather hangings which were painted with trees, birds and flowers. It also had two fine mantelpieces, one inlaid with marquetry and the other of white statuary marble. After the Thew family moved to Stonegate street, no tenant could be found, the property became derelict and these magnificent fittings were sold piecemeal.

Active, energetic and useful

John Dyker Thew was an ardent Conservative. His political career began in 1857, when he was elected to represent the South Ward following the retirement of Mr J. Wales. He held his seat until 1885, when he was appointed an alderman of the borough, a position which he held to the end. Lord Chancellor Cairns appointed him a Justice of the Peace in 1868. He was Mayor three times: in 1871, 1876 and 1885. A founder of Lynn Conservative Club, he reached the peak of his political ambition following the death of Sir Lewis Jarvis in 1888, when he succeeded him as chairman of the Lynn Loyal and Constitutional Association and chieftain of the local Conservative party.

He played an active role in many companies in his efforts to boost the town and trade of Lynn: chairman of the Lynn Gas Company for many years, a director of the Lynn Dock Company from 1877 to 1887, and a director of the East Coast Steam Shipping Company. Despite his best intentions, he was also founder and director of several businesses which failed, including the Town and Country Insurance Company, the Lynn Sea Fisheries Company and the Oil Mill and Seed Crushing Company.

His strong views on many issues brought him into frequent conflict, yet he never sought to oppress or triumph over an adversary. Seeing himself as a guardian of public interests, he unceasingly offered his voice, his purse and his time to advance the prosperity of Lynn and to relieve poverty and suffering. He was an amazingly busy man: a member of the Weekly Board of the West Norfolk and Lynn Hospital; a Charity Trustee; a governor of Elsden

Almshouses; and for a time one of the governors of the Grammar School. He was president of the Working Men's Club and Institute, treasurer of the Freemasons' lodge, and honorary member of the Oddfellows.

A staunch Churchman and regular churchgoer, he was a churchwarden of St Margaret's parish from 1879 to 1885, and honorary secretary to the committee for building St John's church Lynn. He was one of the promoters of the Church of England Young Men's Society and its president for a year or two. It was mainly due to his energy and generosity that this society had a splendid building in which its members could meet.

Hunstanton

In common with many better-off folk at Lynn, John Dyker Thew took a second house at Hunstanton. He became well-known at St Edmund's church and involved himself in the development of the town's railway, gas and water works, and its pier, which was built by his father-in-law, William Smith Simpson. In 1878, he was one of the directors of the Hunstanton Cliff Company Limited, which sought to raise capital of £15,000. His fellow directors included Hamon LeStrange of Hunstanton Hall and William Pattrick of King's Lynn. Their prospectus drew attention to the 'unrivalled beach', the 'invigorating qualities of the air' and the proximity of the resort to the royal residence at Sandringham. A sea wall and esplanade would be constructed; Turkish and swimming baths would be set amongst ornamental gardens, croquet lawns and tennis courts. Pavilions, arbours, seats and shelters would protect against the wind and the rain. They hoped that these facilities would extend the season and attract invalids and convalescents who would be able to enjoy the therapeutic properties of a recently discovered spring, which was richer in iron than John's Well at Harrogate.

Tenor bell tolled

John Dyker Thew had been in poor health for some time when, on 10 September 1891, his third son Percy was struck down at Hunstanton at the age of 36. He and Jane went to Hastings to grieve and to recuperate; they returned to Lynn on Monday 5 October. The following day he took the chair, as President of the Loyal and Constitutional Association, at a meeting which selected Mr T. Gibson Bowles as the Unionist candidate for the borough. The break seemed to have done him good.

A violent gale blew up suddenly on Tuesday 13 October 1891 and swept over the whole of England, reaching the east coast that night. The inhabitants of Lynn awoke to find the streets littered with broken tiles and slates, and the Walks and the Chase strewn with small branches torn from the avenues of trees. Many oaks had been felled by the storm. That Wednesday, as he looked out on the devastation, John Dyker Thew was preparing to take the chair at a great public demonstration in support of Mr Gibson Bowles. On October 15 he went to the office at mid-morning, appearing quite cheerful as he chatted with his friends and colleagues. It was nearly 5 o'clock before he left. Safely home, he collapsed on his dining room floor before he had even removed his coat. Jane summoned help but, although Dr Plowright, Mr S.M.W. Wilson, and Mr G.R. Chadwick arrived swiftly, John Dyker Thew was already dead. Another mighty Lynn oak had fallen and the tenor bell of St Margaret's was tolled.

The funeral procession left the house in Stonegate street shortly before one o'clock on the following Monday. Flags were still at half mast, windows were shaded, and many shops were closed. The coffin was carried to Hardwick Road cemetery in a Washington car, escorted by bearers who were all workmen employed by Messrs Thew & Son: R.W. Wadlow, R.V. Butcher, J.J. Terrington, J.J. Pimbley, E.W. Thorn, W.I. Warnes, W.H. Greeves and E. Emms.

Chapter 7

Fiddaman's hotel

The Wheatsheaf

James Fiddaman was nearly thirty years old when he settled down and built his life at Lynn. The property which would become known as Fiddaman's Hotel, 11 Norfolk street, was owned by Mr. Howlett, a wine and spirit merchant. At the front, the building was three storeys high and to the right hand side there was a long cobbled passage, which took horse drawn carriages and carts to the rear of the premises. Part had been used as offices by the East Anglian Railway Company. In 1850 the property was hired by John Jackson, a Scot, who licensed it for the retail trade and named it the Wheatsheaf. John moved in with his wife Charlotte, a Walpole girl whom he had married ten years earlier, and their five children: John William, Thomas, George Edward, Jane Matilda, and baby William Henry. Three servants also lived on the premises: Mary Ann Marshall, a sixteen year old barmaid from Tilney; and Mary Ann Holding and Mary Claydon, both nineteen year old house maids, from Gaywood and Shouldham respectively.

Baby William Henry died on 20 July 1852. The family were devastated and decided to sell up and move out. The next week, for several weeks, George Mingay sought interest in 'a first rate premises for carrying on the wine and spirit trade, with a retail bar, handsomely fitted up and well situated for trade, being in the centre of the town of Lynn'. On 11 September 1852, Mingay announced the sale by auction of the entire contents on the premises of John Jackson, including a grand piano, the contents of the nursery, all other household furniture, bar fittings, wines and spirits. James Fiddaman recognised the potential of the premises and in September 1852 the license for the Wheatsheaf was transferred to him.

Just over a month later, on 12 November 1852, James married Jemima at St Margaret's church. He signed his name in the marriage register as James 'Francis' Fiddaman, perhaps discarding 'Fidget' in order to emphasise that his days of restless wandering were over and that he intended to make his mark at Lynn. He must have quickly proved himself for he had reverted to 'Fidget' by the time that their first child was born in 1854!

Over the next ten years James and Jemima struggled to build their business in a flurry of entrepreneurial activity and hard work. They promoted dining, invested in the hotel, encouraged patronage by the sporting fraternity, built up the bar trade and off-sales, and diversified into outside catering. When times were hard, James had to engage in some surprising ventures, including a collaboration with fellow innkeepers John Langley, at the Bird in Hand in Norfolk street, and James Crisp, of the Live-and-let-Live in Windsor place, in which they removed night soil, free of cost.

James' and Jemima's labours gradually bore fruit and they were able to purchase the house and adjoining land from Howlett's trustees. They nearly lost their investment on 21 February 1860, when an ember fell from the hearth in one of the lower rooms and ignited the floorboards. Luckily the fire was put out before it caused more extensive damage. By the mid-1860s, they had transformed the Wheatsheaf into Fiddaman's hotel.

These were also the years when James and Jemima struggled to raise a family. Their joy at the birth of Ann Elizabeth in January 1854 was short-lived for she was a sickly child who lived only seven weeks, despite being taken to James' parents' house at Fakenham away from the unhealthy atmosphere of Lynn. In February the following year, their hopes were raised when James was born, only to be dashed five months later when he died of whooping cough. At last there was Frederick, a healthy baby born on 17 April 1856, who lived his childhood at the Wheatsheaf and grew into a fine young man.

Well-aired beds and chops at the shortest notice

James and Jemima set about rivalling the Black Horse, aiming to attract travellers by serving their needs for transport as well as accommodation. They built loose boxes and a lock-up coach-house and acquired horses and gigs for hire. A gentleman who arrived by stage coach or railway could eat well, drink well, and rest overnight in a well-aired bed before rising fresh for business the following morning. Commercial travellers could display their samples to Lynn shopkeepers in rooms at the Wheatsheaf or hire a gig for calls on buyers in the surrounding towns and villages. Farmers could stable their horses while they were at market. All could look forward to an evening spent in pleasant surroundings amongst like-minded fellows.

Jemima quickly became renowned for providing succulent chops and steaks at shortest notice as the Wheatsheaf vied for a share of the lucrative trade serving luncheons and dinners to farmers, shopkeepers and tradesmen. Every market Tuesday at a quarter past one, she served an 'ordinary', a meal prepared at a fixed tariff for all comers. Henry Wanty at the Star inn, only two doors away, was badly hit by her competition and forced to reduce the price of his market dinners to one shilling each. By the 1860s her annual dinners for tradesmen and others were proving exceedingly popular. The Agricultural Dinner on Tuesday 6 March 1860 was held under the slogan 'Speed the Plough'. By half-past five o'clock the dining room was packed with farmers who had each paid 2s 6d. The meal provided a most satisfactory end to a long day at market with plenty of time afterwards for toasts accompanied by cigars and a few glasses of brandy.

Hazards of the hotel trade

James and Jemima were respected as firm but fair employers by their barmaids, cooks and general servants. One of the few who tried to take advantage of them was Henry Wagg, whom they employed on a casual basis in 1872. Around Easter that year they caught him stealing glass tumblers, cruets and salt cellars and he was brought up on remand at Lynn petty sessions. James judged that he had been taught a sufficient lesson and did not appear to press the charge. The magistrates discharged Wagg.

Others were not so fortunate. In 1874 the Christmas poultry outside the kitchen at Fiddaman's provided too great a temptation to J. Wright, a thirty nine year old travelling shoemaker from Chester. It was about half-past nine o'clock on Christmas eve. A brace of pheasants and a considerable quantity of other poultry were hanging at the back of the hotel, either destined for the dinner table or prizes still awaiting collection from that year's draw. Wright entered the passage leading to the wine and spirit vaults and saw the poultry. He took the brace of pheasants, hid them under his coat, and left swiftly in the direction of the Tuesday Market place. Unfortunately PC Taylor, who was standing on a nearby corner, spotted the bulge under his coat and saw the telltale beak of a pheasant hanging below the hem. Wright protested that he had picked them up on the road but PC Taylor saw that the birds' feathers were quite dry despite the streets being damp. Wright was arrested. The theft was quickly traced to Fiddaman's and Jemima identified the pheasants by the special knot which she always tied in the string when she hung poultry. At Lynn petty sessions on Monday 28 December, Wright pleaded guilty to stealing the pheasants, which were valued at 8s. The magistrates were unimpressed by his plea that he stole because he was hard up and sentenced him to 21 days hard labour.

Good taste and style

The Wheatsheaf offered a very wide range of liquid refreshment for consumption both on and off the premises. It benefited from the boom in alcohol consumption which was to reach an all-time peak during the mid-1870s, when annual per capita consumption reached over a gallon of spirits, nearly 35 gallons of beer and half a gallon of wine. Allowing for young children, teetotallers, and those who drank little or infrequently, a high proportion of the population drank prodigious amounts and spent immense sums, usually to the detriment of their families. The deeper the poverty of a town or district the higher was the ratio of public houses to population. In the second half of the nineteenth century Lynn had one public house or beerhouse for every 100 or so inhabitants; nearly twice the national average!

James wanted to attract predominantly middle class customers by offering them good taste and style. He quickly appreciated the potential of Wenham Lake ice which had become a fashionable accompaniment to society's drinks when it was served at Queen Victoria's dinner table. So it was, in the 1860s, that he offered the ice at Fiddaman's hotel and in his refreshment marquees. For a decade or so he became a tiny part of a major industry centred on Wenham, a small town about twenty miles north of Boston, Massachusetts, on the shore of a lake from which natural ice was shipped to Europe and India.

Occasionally a gentleman at 'Fiddy's' hotel would be caught out by the potency of the brandy, as was William Barrett, a seventy year old farmer from Saddlebow, in 1878. On a cold November evening, he had a couple of glasses of brandy and water. He took a wrong turn coming out into the street and went in the direction of the Alexandra dock, where he made three separate attempts to enter but was repulsed on each occasion by the gate keeper, James Hitchcock, who was also about seventy years old. Barrett later charged Hitchcock with assault and the case came before the petty sessions on Monday 2 December. When Edwin Elmer Durrant, one of the magistrates, asked whether he had been perfectly sober, Barrett replied 'Oh yes, sir, quite', at which point there was much laughter in court. The case was dismissed because Barrett was judged to have been 'helplessly drunk'.

Music hall and bowling alley

By 1854 the amusements at the Wheatsheaf included rifle shooting, billiards, quoits, skittles and brasses. That year James decided to take a share in the evening entertainments which had sprung up as an accompaniment to Lynn Races. He obtained special permission from the Mayor to use the Tuesday Market place for a grand public display of fireworks, engaging the 'Pyrotechnical Artiste from the Royal Surrey Zoological Gardens' and promising that the display would exceed those of previous years. Lynn Saxhorn band played popular music in the brilliant moonlight while the crowd were treated to a spectacular show. It opened with a salute of imitation cannon fire, followed by mines of serpents, golden rain, brilliant red, green and purple stars, and several set pieces and concluded with a grand set piece of fiery rotating wheels, coloured stars, Roman candles and batteries of mines.

The many hundreds who turned out to watch were encouraged to go on to a 'Grand Concert & Ball' at the New Vauxhall Saloon, a rustic music hall, which was James' counter to the attractions at the Theatre, the Crown Gardens and the newly built Italian-style Athenaeum. Admission was 6d each and an entire change of artistes was promised for the day of the races. Sometimes known as the Wheatsheaf Saloon or New Vauxhall Concert Hall, this venture prospered for many years. In August 1855, when the Ancient Order of Foresters were holding their High Court Meeting, James engaged the d'Aubans, a family renowned for their national and operatic dances, Vaudeville performances and comic duets. He played to the patriotic fervour engendered by the Crimean War by filling the bill with Mlle Aldina, who sang *The Standard of England*, and Mr Wilson, composer and celebrated tenor, whose song *The Red Coats and Blue*, concluded with:

> At these words the proud Czar will be humble,
> Whenever they're opposed to his view,
> They will tell him that tyranny must crumble
> At the deeds of our Red coats and Blue.

James ensured a steady supply of entertainment and claimed that his saloon was 'equal to any out of London'. He competed with attractions such as the Mart by engaging a more prestigious company. During the Mart in 1858, at half-past seven every evening, Mr W.H. Barry opened the show with his

'Portfolio of Original Fun'. He was the comedian who had the unenviable task of warming up the audience for the star turn: 'Mr and Mrs J. Pete Drice, Ebony Minstrels, Late of Cremorne Gardens and the Egyptian Hall'. They presented their black boy and yellow girl act, which was billed as 'chaste and pleasing entertainment' although unlikely to be judged politically correct by today's standards. The multi-talented Mr Drice also performed his 'never-to-be-forgotten heel-tapping jig in a style peculiar to himself'. Musical accompaniment was provided by a brass and string band led by Mr W. Dace. Admission was 3d, except on Tuesdays when admission was raised to 6d.

James never lost an opportunity to provide new attractions at the Wheatsheaf. He was also quick to grasp every opportunity for extra publicity and extra sales, as he showed in 1858, when he added a bowling alley to the premises. He announced in the *Lynn Advertiser*, under the heading 'Royal, Loyal', that his 'splendid bowling alley, not to be equalled in England' had been built 'at great expense' and would be opened on Monday 25 June 'to celebrate the wedding of the young Princess' - the marriage of Queen Victoria's eldest daughter Victoria, the Princess Royal, to the crown prince of Prussia.

Hospital and Mart Balls

James and Jemima extended their catering business beyond Fiddaman's hotel. At the beginning they provided refreshments outdoors in booths or marquees, frequently at rustic gatherings and often in partnership with John J. Lowe. They gradually earned a reputation for style and liberality which eventually made them a natural choice for many civic events.

There were evening dinners at the Town Hall when the Mayor entertained members of the council and a few invited guests, as did John Osborne Smetham in January 1882 after an annual audit of the corporation accounts. And there were the two balls held annually around the time of the Mart. One was to raise funds for the West Norfolk and Lynn Hospital, popularly known as the Hospital Ball and held on a Tuesday; the other was held on the following Thursday by the Mayor and was known as the Mart Ball. Both occupied the Assembly Rooms at the Town Hall and invariably used the Stone Hall as a reception, refreshment and retiring room. Both were prominent on the calendar of Lynn society.

There was keen competition to cater for these events. Sometimes the contracts would go to two different caterers, as in 1875 when Mr Pollard of the Crown Hotel served the Hospital Ball and James Fiddaman the Mart Ball, although Mr Bray's band played at both. Sometimes one caterer would win both contracts as did James Fiddaman in 1878 when 'the decorations were in a more than usually elaborate style' and the music was provided by Messrs Howletts' band from Norwich.

Attendance dropped off considerably through the 1870s. One of the best attendances at the Hospital Ball was in 1867 when about 200 danced to Mr Bray's band until 4 o'clock in the morning. The Mart Ball that year attracted 170, including members of most of the principal families in the neighbourhood. Attendance at the Hospital Ball had dropped to 110 by 1875; only 80 were present in 1878. The Mart Ball still managed to attract 170 in 1872 but slumped to 98 in 1878. Tickets for both events in 1878 were quite reasonably priced at 7s each, so what caused this decline? 'Old Sir Roger' offered his explanation in a letter to the *Lynn Advertiser* on 2 March 1878, blaming the divisions that existed between town and country, trade and gentry, and age and youth:

> .. of late years a certain 'clique' have arrogated to themselves the monopoly of the greater part of the ball room, and by their unseemly behaviour, and high jinks, looking with contemptuous scorn upon any of their less 'aristocratic' neighbours who should dare to venture amongst their 'set'. It is a notorious fact that this is the reason why so many of the respectable old townsfolk (who may not lay claim to country gentryship) and tradespeople now abstain from intruding their presence amongst their betters (?) and thus a charitable institution, in the case of the first named assembly, suffers, through one of the worst of human weaknesses, 'pride'. In times gone by, it was the custom to see the good old country squires present, followed by a string of their admiring tenants, joining together in the light fantastic step, when all was mirth and good humour. Alas! all this has fled, and only the 'swells' in their red coats, to make believe they are all MFHs, with their immediate friends have now the entrée.

Chapter 8

John J Lowe

Family

John Joseph Lowe was born at Lynn in 1826, the first child of Joseph Lowe and Frances née Brown. In 1829 his sister Harriett was born; and in 1831 his brother Frederick Browne. A year or so later Joseph died and in 1837 Frances remarried to Robert Fayers, a baker. The Fayers lived in Church street just down the road from the Three Tunns inn where John J. and James Fiddaman were to forge their lifelong friendship.

John J. Lowe became a master baker and married Matilda Burcham in 1849. One of the witnesses was Thomas Springall, keeper of the Black Horse in Chapel street at that time. John J. and Matilda had three daughters, Frances (Fanny) in 1850, Matilda in 1852 and Harriett Ann in 1854.

In 1872 Frances married Thomas William Blomfield (1849-1907), a ship's officer who was best known in later life as a hay and corn merchant but whose hectic business affairs encompassed licensee of the Princess Royal in Blackfriars street, proprietor of Blackfriars Street Stores, tobacconist at 7 St James street, cattle canvasser for the Great Eastern Railway, farmer and proprietor of Blomfield's weighbridge in Blackfriars street. By 1905 he was styling himself as 'Corn Merchant by appointment to His Majesty the King, St John's Terrace'. Frances produced six girls during the first ten years of their marriage, one of whom died in infancy. Then on 25 March 1883 a son was born; he was called Thomas and was given the middle name Fiddaman in honour of his godfather James Fiddaman. During the next ten years Frances gave birth to another three girls and then a boy; the last two died in childhood.

Black Horse hotel

John J. took over the Black Horse in 1859 and continued to run it as an hotel. His guests were travellers and craftsmen. His staff at that time included William Hunt, a middle-aged porter, and three servants Eliza Cooper, Ann Thurrell and Matthew Shaw, all of whom were around twenty years old. Perhaps his most famous guest was Joseph Sadler, the celebrated sculler of

Black Horse hotel in Chapel street
Photograph courtesy of True's Yard Fishing Museum

Putney who chose the Black Horse as his training headquarters for the great race in September 1867 against James Percy of Newcastle upon Tyne. James D. Digby of Lynn had heard that Sadler had challenged Percy to a 2 mile race for £200 a side, Sadler offering £15 for travelling expenses to Percy if the race were to be held on the Thames and being prepared to take the same amount to row on the Tyne. Digby immediately wrote to both men offering to raise £20 towards their expenses if the match were rowed at Lynn. His offer was accepted, the *Sportsman* held the stake money of £400, and subscribers at Lynn quickly contributed over £15 towards the expenses. James Fiddaman secured the banks of the Cut for the afternoon of Wednesday the 18th and set about promoting some local races, although it was only three months since the King's Lynn Royal Regatta. Sadler arrived at the Black Horse two weeks before the event with an entourage which included his mentor, Edward May of Barnes, and William Sadler. Percy arrived only a few days before the race and set up his headquarters at the Portland Arms. The great day arrived; the wind was against an ebb tide and the water was choppy. There was a good crowd of locals, sportsmen and Londoners taking advantage of the refreshment booths as they watched the seven supporting events. The challenge was the last race of the day. Spectators on the west bank of the Cut lined the whole length of the course. The betting at the start was 5 to 4 on

Sadler. Sadler won the toss and chose the west station, which was the more sheltered. Just before 6 o'clock they were off. Although Percy took an early lead, Sadler's daily training on the Ouse paid dividends and he came home to win by several lengths.

Moderately successful businessman

John J. ran several other businesses: providing a carrier service to London; supplying hay and corn to customers in the town and surrounding country. He had a thriving catering business in his own right and was also very active in partnership with James Fiddaman. The marquee of 'Fiddaman & Lowe' was a familiar sight at Volunteers camps and the Royal Regatta.

When he died on 15 April 1898 he left an estate valued at about £2,400. His brother Frederick Browne Lowe received 10 guineas for acting as a trustee. His wife Matilda was a trustee and the principal beneficiary until her death, when the estate was split between the three daughters: Frances the wife of Thomas William Blomfield; Matilda the wife of Joseph Warner of Nottingham; and Harriett Ann the wife of George Holdcross.

Chapter 9

Sporting house

Malodorous reputation

Gambling was widespread in the mid-nineteenth century and was not confined to the turf, being commonplace in sports such as rowing and athletics. Wagers were also an inevitable accompaniment to entertainment at inns and taverns. James Fiddaman's advertisement for the Wheatsheaf in Blomfield's 1856 *Directory of Norfolk* offered a wide choice: 'billiard room, pleasure gardens, and large ground where quoits, skittles, rifle shooting, and other games and various athletic sports, too numerous for an advertisement, are constantly practised'.

James transformed the Wheatsheaf into Fiddaman's hotel as he played an increasingly influential role in the organisation of sporting events at Lynn. He began with pigeon shooting matches in the 1850s, prospered in the 1860s with the revival of horse racing at Lynn Races and Royal patronage of Lynn Regatta, and his crowning glory was the creation of Lynn Gala in 1868. He was a natural target for the disapproval of the 'respectable' citizens of Lynn, who read frequently about the violence and hooliganism at race meetings organised by publicans and bookmakers, whose sole purpose was to draw crowds to bet and drink beer! It was this shadier side of his life and his hotel which were highlighted by the *Lynn News* in his obituary:

> In the earlier time of its establishment, the hotel was especially known as a sporting house. Mr Fiddaman had intimate relations with the racing fraternity, and his hotel was a centre of local betting and other sporting transactions. There were some circumstances which at the period we are referring to gave a malodorous reputation to Mr Fiddaman's house; but in the course of time the hotel assumed a better character.

Pedestrianism ...

The Wheatsheaf always had something out of the ordinary to grab the attention of a sport, like the week in September 1853 when A. Elson attempted to walk sixty miles each day for six successive days. This slight eighteen year old, a few inches over five feet tall and weighing less than seven and a half stone, appealed to a generous public to reward him if he should be successful. Each day he set out from the Wheatsheaf via Swaffham to the Lord Nelson at East Dereham and back, returning to sleep at the Wheatsheaf before eight o'clock at night. In a single stroke, James gained valuable publicity and was virtually guaranteed extra custom every night that week, not to mention the opportunities for taking wagers or running a book on the outcome. Much to everyone's surprise, Elson triumphed. Both he and James must have been rewarded handsomely for he returned a year or so later to attempt 100 miles in 24 hours for a wager of £10. On this occasion he started from the Wheatsheaf inn at 6 o'clock on Thursday evening and was due to finish there at the same time on the next day.

...and pigeon shooting

For over twenty years from the 1850s, James organised pigeon shooting matches. The rules required guns to be less than 10-bore, loaded with 1 1/2 oz. shot, and only one barrel to be used. Live pigeons were released from a basket, or trap, at a range of 21 or 22 yards and were allowed as hits only if they fell within sixty yards. Sparrows provided a smaller target and were therefore released at a range of only 18 yards. Competitors were required to hold their guns below the elbow in a sportsmanlike manner until the pigeon or sparrow was on the wing. Keen rivalry was guaranteed by pitting town against country, perhaps a Lynn gentleman against a Marshland gentleman, each of whom would place a stake of £10 or £20 and sometimes as much as £50, winner take all. James acted as stakeholder and was ideally placed to enter into transactions with spectators who might wish to place bets on the outcomes. One of the first matches took place on the Lynn Cricket ground on Wednesday 9 August 1854 between Mr Charles Gay of Lynn and Mr Moore of Foulsham. The contest began at one o'clock and must have been soon over since each man had only eleven birds to target. On this occasion the shooting was considered not good on either side; Gay was the victor, killing six birds to his opponents' five. The public, who had been charged 3d each for admission, were disappointed.

In April the following year, James succeeded in recapturing public interest with his 'Pigeon Shooting Extraordinary'. Three matches between gentlemen were followed by sweepstakes, with plentiful supplies of pigeons and sparrows, and admission was charged at only 2d each. The sweepstakes were most popular with field sportsmen who were keen to prove their prowess for individual stakes which might be anything from 2s 6d to £1. James' shooting matches became annual fixtures, usually at the Cricket Field near Hardwick road but sometimes in a field near the Lynn Union workhouse. The sport invariably lasted until it was almost dark, when competitors and spectators alike retired to the Wheatsheaf for a dinner, which was good value at two shillings per head and often featured Jemima's renowned pigeon pies. By 1869 James had teamed up with John J. Lowe to provide refreshments throughout the contests.

Courtesy of King's Lynn Museums

Sweepstakes and draws

Sweepstakes were illegal under legislation prohibiting lotteries but flourished in the mid-nineteenth century when they were advertised in *Bell's Life* and other sporting publications. The practice declined when the Attorney-General threatened that he would prosecute any newspaper publishing a sweepstake advertisement. The 'Great St Leger Distribution' at King's Lynn in 1865 seems to have overcome these obstacles. This was one of the ventures of James D. Digby, of 9 Buckingham terrace, Lynn, a gentleman with whom James was to have a disagreement about Lynn Races in 1868. An advertisement in the *Lynn Advertiser* announced that seven thousand tickets were for sale at 1s each by James Digby and his agents: James Fiddaman and Henry Spencer at Lynn; William Campling of The Cambridge, Haymarket at Norwich; Mr Regester at Wisbech; and William Allen at Thornham. Whoever drew the winner of the St Leger received a prize of £75; £25 was offered for the second, £10 for the third, 30s for every starter, and 5s for each non-starter. Less than half of the £350 proceedings was paid out as prize money. The agents earned a few pennies for each ticket sold and shared about £100 while James Digby took £100 for his risks as promoter.

James Fiddaman's own draws were generous in comparison. At Christmas time it was customary for inns to hold a draw for prizes; and the Wheatsheaf was no exception. James' first Christmas draw was held in 1855 and the event was still going strong some fifteen years later. In 1858 the event was a 'Christmas Treat' and 'shares' at 1s each were offered to four thousand 'subscribers', whose interests were safeguarded by a committee who conducted the draw. There were 1,000 prizes, including a splendid fat pig, which was probably given to James as a piglet, by one of his farmer friends, and fattened by Jemima on leftovers! In 1866 he also promoted an 'Easter Distribution', prompted by friends, one of whom wished to dispose of the major prize: a nearly new four-wheel carriage built by Hunnybun of Cambridge at a cost of £50, complete with cob horse and harness. There were sixty prizes in all, including: two magnificent musical boxes made by the celebrated Nicole Freres; three elegant dressing cases, including one made by Mappin & Co, in rosewood with silver fittings; a handsome gilt timepiece; several gallons of brandy, rum, gin and whiskey; dozens of wines; and boxes of cigars. 5,000 subscribers paid 1s each to enter. As usual the draw was under the management of a committee of gentlemen; the successful numbers and a description of each prize were published in the *Lynn Advertiser*. By 1869 the 'Christmas Club' was promoted in partnership with John J. Lowe. The prizes included eight fat bullocks, three fat sheep, a very valuable brown cob and 100 other valuable articles, all to be seen at Fiddaman's hotel. On this occasion there were 5,000 'members' who were offered 'vouchers' at 2s each, or at a discount of 6 for 11s, 12 for 20s or 25 for 40s. James made a good profit on the draws, not least because he paid trade prices for all the prizes. Presumably his subscribers, or members, must have judged the draws to be fair, for they returned year after year for over fifteen years.

Racing fraternity

When James took over the Wheatsheaf in 1852, it was perfectly lawful for a bookmaker to post lists of the odds and to take cash bets from all and sundry. Such betting was outlawed by an Act of Parliament in 1853 because it was believed that it exposed working men to unacceptable temptation and had led too many of them into lives of crime. Gentlemen, of course, could still place off-course bets on credit. The Act succeeded only in driving the activity underground, where it continued to flourish, working men placing their bets via newsagents' or barbers' shops, in public houses, or in the streets. It seems that neither the threat nor the reality of prosecution did much to deter the business.

James welcomed gentlemen to Fiddaman's hotel, particularly those with an interest in the turf. He showed it in the papers which he offered them: not only the *Morning Advertiser, Standard, Telegraph*, and, of course, the *Lynn Advertiser*, but also *Bell's Life, Punch, Town Talk, Illustrated London News, Racing Times*, and *Feist's* and *Rough's Guide to the Turf*. He installed and staffed sophisticated facilities for singeing and clipping gentlemen's horses. In the season his stables played host to stallions at stud. In March 1859, it was *The Tester*, a dark brown thoroughbred by *Melbourne* out of *Pickledust*, six years old, and standing fifteen hands and three inches high, owned by William Spikings, of Wingland near Wisbech. The stallion's pedigree sounded impressive, being half-brother to several winners of the 2,000 Guineas, Derby, Oaks and St Leger. The fee was 5 guineas for a thoroughbred mare and 2 guineas for a half-bred mare, with 2s 6d for the services of the groom. Thoroughbred mares which had won a purse of £200 were served free of charge. *The Tester* exhibited considerable stamina following a circuit for several weeks, each day journeying fifteen or twenty miles and serving mares at several villages along the way. Wisbech to Lynn on Mondays, staying overnight in James Fiddaman's stables at the Wheatsheaf. On Tuesdays moving on to the Wheatsheaf at Heacham; Wednesdays to the Swan inn, Massingham; Thursdays to the Bell inn, Marham; Fridays to the Swan inn, Outwell; and Saturdays back to Wisbech. Sunday was a day of rest.

Blood sports

Cockfighting was popular at Lynn in the late eighteenth century and its popularity continued well into the early nineteenth century, despite the passing of a law in 1849 which made it an offence even on private premises. Mr Collins Webber Langwade, the manager at Fiddaman's hotel from about 1942, used to tell his son, Michael, that once upon a time cockfights had been staged at the rear of the premises. There was a room in the wine and spirits stores which was about 25 ft square, having a raised platform on three sides which was just wide enough to stand two rows of people. There is no evidence that James did promote cockfights, or any other blood sports, but animal blood was certainly spilt one summer evening in 1878.

At about six o'clock on Tuesday 23 July, the bar was quite full. Amongst others, there were: William Leeds, a dealer of Longham, and his father; Henry Rix, a Dersingham farmer; Mr Norris; Mr Gardiner; James Rippingale of Flitcham; and Watts Tann, a horse-breaker of West Lynn. Mr Scott entered with his two year old dog, which played about the bar, while he sat drinking. Tann and Leeds were sitting close together. They picked up the dog and played with it behind their backs. The dog suddenly 'shruck' out, was thrown down by Tann, and ran about the bar shrieking and tail-less. The barmaid, Emily Hollingsworth, saw the distressed dog, and its blood on the floor, and called James Fiddaman. James was disgusted by the cowardly act. He asked who had cut off the tail and immediately offered a reward of £5 for the discovery of the culprits. Tann and Leeds left immediately. There was blood where they had been sitting and the tail was found underneath the seat. Superintendent George Ware was called. James Rippingale was the only witness to the whole proceedings and even he had not actually seen the tail removed. Leeds' father left the house to warn his son, closely followed by Supt Ware. At the Sun, further along Norfolk street, Supt Ware found Tann, still with blood on one of his hands and wet blood stains on his coat tails. Tann denied harming the dog and argued that the blood was from a horse which he had been cutting. Despite his protests, he was arrested 'red-handed'. Supt Ware caught up with Leeds at Gaywood, by which time he had changed his clothes. The two men appeared at Lynn petty sessions on Monday 29 July before the Mayor, and George Holditch, Robert Henry Household and John G. Wigg Esqs. The court room was packed and a small crowd of disappointed people waited, ears pricked, in the lobby outside. Mr Wilkin prosecuted, arguing strongly for the maximum sentence of three months imprisonment with hard labour if the accused should be proved guilty of such 'a barbarous and wanton piece of cruelty ..... upon a poor little harmless dog'. Mr S. Linay, of Sadd and Linay, Norwich, defended, arguing that the evidence was purely circumstantial, no knife or scissors had been found, and that Rippingale was unreliable because he only wished to claim the £5 reward. The magistrates decided that the case had been proved; they fined Watts Tann £5 with £4 9s 6d costs and William Leeds £5 with £3 17s 6d costs.

Chapter 10

Civic celebrations

Crimean War and peace

Turkey declared war against Russian aggression in 1853; Britain and France sided with Turkey and declared war on Russia in March the following year. So began the Crimean War, which was to last two years. Income tax had stood at 7d in the pound but was promptly doubled to help pay for the war. These were difficult times for James and Jemima, coming to terms with the loss of their first child, Ann Elizabeth, and, within a year, having to endure the loss of a second, James, soon after his birth. They were nervously awaiting the birth of their third child while peace terms were being negotiated at the Congress of Paris in March 1856. Frederick, a healthy baby, arrived on 17 April and peace was proclaimed two weeks later.

In the immediate aftermath of the war, there was no great enthusiasm for celebrating the peace, neither at Lynn nor in the rest of the country. The Town Council were set against a public celebration, although they did order church bells to be rung. However, public sentiment grew steadily in favour of commemorating the peace. The Mayor took a lead with the arrangements and declared Wednesday 21 May a holiday.

The celebrations were heralded by a brilliant sunrise, firing of guns and ringing of the church bells. Flags, bunting and banners fluttered in the streets; ships in the harbour flew their colours. At midday over two thousand flag waving children assembled in the Tuesday Market place, each wearing a souvenir name badge. In the centre of the square, Lynn Saxhorn band, in stylish uniform caps, struck up the 'National Anthem' and the children sang a chorus. Cannon fire reverberated from Common Staith quay, signalling the start of a march to the Walks. Led by the band and accompanied by dense crowds, the procession extended over half a mile.

Masterminded by Frederic Kendle, the Walks had been decorated with flags, strung from tree to tree. Three parallel rows of trestle tables had been constructed, each row over 200 yards long and covered with snow-white calico. Mrs Batterbee, keeper of the Town Hall and wife of the town gaoler, had supervised the preparation of 2000 lb of plum pudding, 1000 lb of roast beef and 1000 lb of bread. While the children tucked in, the band played 'The Roast Beef of Old England'. After grace and three cheers for 'the Queen and the Royal Family', 'the Peace and those who won it' and 'the Mayor', the children marched to Goodwin's Fields, where they played for the rest of the day. That night the Mayor enjoyed dinner and elegant and luxurious entertainment at the Globe, in the company of forty prominent citizens, including Walter Moyse, Lewis Whincop Jarvis, and John Dyker Thew. At the Athenaeum another sixty gentlemen enjoyed dinner served by Mr Marshall of the Duke's Head hotel.

Detail from 'The Peace commemoration at Lynn-schoolchildrens' festival, in the public Walks'
The *Illustrated London News* June 7, 1865

Wedding of the Prince of Wales, 1863

Just after noon on Saturday 7 March 1863, Princess Alexandra was landing at Gravesend. At St Ann's fort Lynn, a group of artillerymen marked the moment by firing the Sebastopol gun, which had been transported on a specially constructed carriage from its stone pedestal near the Athenaeum. The charge was small and the resulting detonation was disappointing, only just being heard at South Quay where the corporation guns answered with a royal salute. The artillerymen decided to use a much larger charge next time! St Margaret's bells began to peal and continued to do so at intervals throughout the day.

Ships in the harbour were dressed overall and flags floated from Grey Friar's tower, the South Gates, Town Hall and Custom house as the town's residents and shopkeepers put the finishing touches to their own decorations. In every street they displayed their patriotism and joy at the royal event. There were ensigns, standards and signals of every shape and size, flying from poles and hung by cords. Pennants, banners and streamers fluttered in the breeze. English and Danish national flags dominated the scene, red, white and blue of every hue, punctuated by royal standards emblazoned with gold. High street was festooned from end to end. There were myriad inscriptions. Simple greetings and heartfelt wishes: 'Alexandra, welcome' and 'Health and happiness to the Royal pair'. Some elaborate sentiments: 'God bless the Prince and his Royal bride; may their union be long and happy' beside the Unitarian chapel; and Messrs Bagge's premises in King street proclaimed 'God, the best maker of all marriages, combine your hearts in one'. Outside the Wheatsheaf in Norfolk street James Fiddaman had hung a handsome red banner showing the Prince of Wales' feathers in white alongside another wishing 'Prosperity to the town and trade of Lynn'!

Procession

The wedding day, Tuesday 10 March, dawned with an overcast sky. Signal guns were fired at first light, the church bells began to peal and crowds poured into the town. At 9.30 the Sebastopol gun boomed out from the fort and the head of the procession assembled along the west and north sides of the Tuesday Market place, spilling over into St Nicholas' street. Odd Fellows, Ancient Foresters and members of other friendly societies, some in ceremonial dress but all wearing sashes and carrying banners, waited around the corner in Chapel street. Others waited in Austin street: sworn meters, the guardians of weights and measures, carrying a standard bushel decorated with flowers, evergreens and a silk royal standard; master mariners; sailors and boys carrying models of ships; porters; fishermen and boys carrying nets; and finally the Fire Brigade carrying axes, mounted on an engine drawn by two horses and driven by a scarlet coated outrider. Police Superintendent Cornelius W. Reeves was in charge, assisted by Captain Samuel Cresswell, RN and Edward Bagge, all three on horseback, marshalling the contingents into position.

The Corporation met at the home of the Mayor, Lewis Whincop Jarvis, on Tuesday Market place. The Rifle Corps mounted guard outside and their band played the Danish national anthem. At 9.50 the Sebastopol gun boomed out for a second time. The Mayor and Corporation took their place in the parade and the Chapel street contingent moved into St Nicholas street. Those waiting in Austin street surged forward, impatient to follow. At 10 o'clock the Sebastopol gun boomed out for a third time. Supt Reeves on horseback, resplendent in a blue and white sash and escorted by his men, led the way into King street, followed by the Saxhorn band, wearing red and white caps symbolising the Danish flag. Close on their heels was Major Campbell on horseback, leading the Enrolled Pensioners. Next were the Coastguard and the Royal Navy Volunteers, commanded by Lieut Brooman, RN. The town crier and sergeants at mace, carrying the Corporation sword, maces and banner, preceded the Mayor and Corporation. Then came the borough magistrates and the masters of the Grammar school, clergy, and dissenting ministers, all wearing their academic caps and gowns. The Chapel street contingent came next and that from Austin street brought up the rear. The Rifle Corps did not join in, perhaps fearing for the precision of their marching in such motley company; they held their own parade at the Cricket field, Austin street, which had been loaned by John J. Lowe.

The procession wended its way past the Custom House into Queen street, by St Margaret's church into Church street, down Bridge street, All Saints' street and Valinger's road to the London road. At the South Gates it was joined by the schoolchildren before retracing its steps down London road and via St James' and High streets back to the Tuesday Market place. Here the Corporation, clergy and other ministers mounted a platform at the centre of the square. The bands played while the rest of the procession formed into concentric squares with flag-waving schoolchildren on the inside. Spectators crowded pavements, house windows, and roofs.

Frederick Fiddaman, nearly seven years old, listened fascinated as the town crier called for silence, the Mayor announced the marriage and the Rev Hankinson blessed the Royal couple. The silence was suddenly broken by the Sebastopol gun and rifle salutes. John Henry Pratt, four years old, later recalled that 'the noise of volleys fired by the Volunteers on the Tuesday Market frightened me considerably'.

Detail from 'Lynn: proclamation of the Royal marriage by the Mayor'
The *Illustrated London News,* Supplement, April 4, 1863

Feasting

The publicans and hotel keepers of Lynn had a field day. Mr Johnson of the Mermaid and Mr Elliott of the Three Pigeons shared the contract to supply dinner to over 900 of the aged poor at the Corn Exchange at midday. They had been allowed 2s per person to provide 1 lb. of meat, 1/2 lb. of pudding, as much bread as called for, and 2 pints of beer for a man or 1 pint for a woman. Each man also received 1/2 oz. of tobacco. It was a tight budget; fortuitously the women outnumbered the men by three to two. The guests sat at twelve long tables, which were covered with white cloth and decorated with flowers, each with a president and three assistants to supervise the carving. Forty volunteers waited on the tables. The guests had been required to bring their own knives, forks and pint mugs.

Nearly 3,500 schoolchildren were treated to lunch in their school rooms. The allowance in their case was 1s per head and arrangements were left to the managers of each school. Every child was given a wedding rosette and a commemorative card printed in colour by Mr Taylor of High street.

Rustic sports

After their duties in the Market place and drilling at the Cricket field, the

Rifle Corps had developed healthy appetites. They marched back to the Cricket field where Dr Lowe, their honorary surgeon, treated them to a substantial lunch served by John J. Lowe of the Black Horse. They ended the meal drinking toasts to the health of the royal couple and to Dr Lowe. Spectators soon began arriving for the Rustic Sports, which John J. Lowe had organised for that afternoon, and the Rifle Corps band moved on to play Mendelssohn's Wedding March outside the Mayor's house at two o'clock. Their efforts were much appreciated by the Mayor, who rewarded them liberally with wine.

Crowds poured into the Cricket field in such numbers that it proved exceedingly difficult to keep the oval race track clear. Waggons had been placed alongside the track to give ladies and children a grandstand view, a privilege for which they had to pay 6d. The luncheon booths, which had been occupied earlier by the Rifle Corps, were now open to the public.
John J. Lowe was not one to miss an opportunity. Richard Whitwell, a local veterinary surgeon, was the judge for the sports, W.H. Row was the starter and Mr Wilkin was clerk of the course. The first event was the donkey race and the Mayor, Lewis Whincop Jarvis, had high hopes for his *Don Quixote*, ridden by 'a good looking little fellow, completely got up in buckskin tights, coloured jacket and cap'. Unfortunately he only managed third place behind Mr Rose's *Jack* and James Beckington's *Prince*. The three foot races over 400 yards all drew good entries, with prizes of 20s, 10s and 5s for first, second and third places. Robert Bailey won the fishermen's race, while Edward Hewitt and William Bailey took the places. William Stafford came first in the porters' race, followed by Richard Colman and Charles Morris. Gerard Cresswell, younger brother of Frank and Samuel Cresswell, won the race for members of the Rifle Corps in 59 seconds, followed closely by John Holmes and Alfred Jones. Gerard was victorious again in the 600 yards over three hurdles open to all England, winning a prize of 40s; Whatley Paviour took second place and 20s; John Holmes took third place and 10s.

The sack race had just been run when the heavens opened. Heavy rain and sleet fell for over an hour, driving spectators from the field. It was decided that the wheelbarrow race, pig hunt, and climbing the greasy poles should be postponed. So ended the Rustic Sports, a precursor to the Lynn Gala which John J. Lowe and James Fiddaman would inaugurate some years later.

More feasting

Feasting resumed that evening, to the delight of publicans and hotel keepers. At the Globe hotel Mrs Clayton provided 24 tenants of the Sandringham estate with dinner at the invitation of the Prince of Wales. In the Music Hall at the Athenaeum, over 200 smartly-dressed male and female assistants assembled for a substantial repast served by Mr Cross of the Green Dragon, followed by dancing until four o'clock the following morning. Eighty guests enjoyed a dinner for 3s prepared by a committee of ladies in the Stepney school room.

The sworn meters had enjoyed lunch at the Town Arms before they adjourned to their office to entertain the merchants who relied on their impartial services. They mixed about 8 gallons of rum, brandy and water in equal quantities in one of their bushel measures and enlivened the brew with sugar, lemon juice and spices. The resulting punch was much appreciated by the Mayor and Corporation and about 200 other gentlemen during the course of the evening. The sworn meters enjoyed their supper at the Town Hall while the Mayor and about sixty guests sat down to the public dinner in the Assembly room next door. John Dyker Thew was amongst the guests who enjoyed a five course banquet, washed down with champagne, hock, sherry and port, and accompanied by music from Mr Bray's Quadrille band.

Meanwhile, at the Albion hall in Broad street, James Fiddaman served dinner to about 130 members and guests of the Rifle Corps who had purchased tickets at 8s each. Captain Frank Cresswell was in the chair and his brother Captain Samuel Cresswell, RN was one of the guests. Dr Lowe said grace after dinner before the tables were cleared in preparation for drinking the health of the Queen, the Army and Navy, the Ladies, etc.. Captain Frank Cresswell responded to the toast to his own health by reminding his men that 'If the Corps would only come to drill as they came to dinner they would be a very pleasant company (laughter), and if they used their bayonets as well as they did their forks no foe would venture to come near them (laughter)'.

The weather that evening was clear. Thousands wandered the streets enjoying the illuminations, making their way to Tuesday Market place where the Saxhorn band was playing before the fireworks display at nine o'clock. Frederick Fiddaman thrilled to the cannon fire and sky rockets.

Chapter 11
Francis Joseph Cresswell

Quaker roots

Francis, known as Frank, was born 1 November 1822, the eldest son of Francis Cresswell and Rachel. His maternal grandmother was Elizabeth Fry, a Quaker who devoted her life to prison reform after a visit to Newgate prison in 1813 when she saw the appalling conditions in which 300 women and their children were living. Elizabeth's father was John Gurney, a rich Quaker banker. The family lived at King's Staith square. Frank was educated at Harrow before entering the army as an ensign in the 26th Cameronians in late 1842. He resigned his commission in 1846 and began work in the family banking firm of Messrs Gurneys Birkbeck and Cresswell, later Gurneys and Co, at Lynn. His father died in 1851 and he took his father's place as a partner. In August 1850 he married Charlotte Frances Georgiana, daughter of Lord Calthorpe, by whom he had two sons and two daughters.

Brother Samuel

Frank's brother Samuel Gurney Cresswell joined the Royal Navy and served as a lieutenant on board *H.M.S. Agincourt*, the flagship of Sir Thomas Cochrane, Commander-in-Chief of the East India and China station. Between 1845 and 1847, he distinguished himself in several actions against pirates in Borneo and Brunei. In 1848 he volunteered for Arctic duty and served the next five years on board the *Investigator,* searching unsuccessfully for Sir John Franklin, whose expedition had vanished while exploring for a navigable route between the Atlantic and the Pacific oceans - the North-West passage. After the *Investigator* became trapped in the ice of Mercy bay just north of Banks island, Lieut Cresswell was sent with a sledging party across the frozen ocean to Beechey Island with despatches for the Admiralty. By an incredible stroke of luck they encountered the *Phoenix* under the command of Captain Inglefield, who brought them back to Scotland. Thus Lieut Cresswell's party were credited with being the first to traverse the North-West passage.

On 26 October 1853, Lynn fêted Lieut Cresswell's achievement at a lavish banquet in the Assembly room, tickets 1 guinea each. The Town Clerk read out a 'Congratulatory Address' and the Mayor, Lionel Self, presented him with a copy on an illuminated scroll of vellum to which the Corporate seal was attached by a golden cord. Lieut Cresswell rose to the rank of captain but his years in the Arctic wastes had ruined his health and he died on 14 August 1867 at Bank house, his mother's home, aged only 39 years.

Brother Gerard

The Prince of Wales purchased the Sandringham estate in 1861 and set about indulging his passion for shooting by turning it into one of the most prolific game estates in Europe. Frank's younger brother Gerard and his wife Louise were tenants of Appleton farm, part of the Sandringham estate. Work on their farm was an incessant struggle against the ravages of game reared for shooting parties. Pheasants ate the grain and hares destroyed the mangolds. In the shooting season, work had to stop for two days a week, while their labourers became beaters. Gerard was a fit young man in March 1863 when he took first places in the 400 yards flat and 600 yards hurdles races at John J. Lowe's 'Rustic Sports'. However, the farm was barely profitable and a constant worry. Joy at the birth of daughter Frances Dorothea in April 1863 turned to despair when she died in January the following year. Despite the birth of baby Gerard in October 1864, the stress took its toll and Gerard died at the age of 28 in 1865.

Frank, who was an executor of his brother's will, helped Louise in her fight for compensation for crop damage from the Prince of Wales. They withheld rent until damages were eventually agreed at about £500. With a young son to support, Louise managed the farm single-handed. In 1869 she reared some fox cubs as a favour to Edmund Beck, the new agent for Sandringham estate. At the time over seventy pheasants in surrounding plantations were killed by foxes and the head keeper blamed Louise's cubs. Louise argued that it was more likely to have been an old fox. Edmund Beck supported her. The keeper was quietly transferred to a post at Windsor where he allegedly became a close friend of John Brown.

Wild Duck

Frank's leisure time was spent close to the Ouse and the Wash. He was a keen fisherman and enjoyed hunting ducks, using nets to snare them, but his great love was boats and boating. He was a member of the Royal Thames Yacht Club and an Associate of the Society of Naval Architects. He designed, constructed and raced several yachts, all named *Wild Duck*, with the assistance of Henry Hornigold, his yachtsman. His fourth *Wild Duck* was built by W. Whall at West Lynn: just over 52 ft long with a beam of 12 ft 6 in and displacement of 27 tons. Her hull was made of two inch thick planks of English oak. Samuel Parker of South quay provided the masts; Charles Seapy Dawes, the blacksmith in Priory lane, forged the iron work. Miss Gurney launched her in March 1878.

Frank regularly raced his yachts in the Lynn Roads regattas of the 1850s and '60s and was disappointed when the event lapsed. He was jovial and hearty, always ready to organise sport and entertainment for the pleasure and enjoyment of others, so it was no surprise when he was one of the small group of gentlemen who decided to revive Lynn sailing regatta in 1872. They raised funds for the King's Lynn Challenge Cup, to the Lynn Well light and back, value 30 guineas plus entry money and open to yachts of any rig belonging to Lynn or Boston. A second event for a purse of £5 for fishing boats was abandoned because there were too few entries. On 22 July there was a good breeze from the south-south-east. Eight yachts lay moored by their sterns in the river, off the entrance of the Alexandra dock, awaiting the start from Mr Playford. *Amateur*, owned by J.H. Garfit and A.H. Staniland of Boston, crossed the starting line before the first gun and was immediately disqualified by the judge, James Bowker, who was on board a Trinity pilot cutter with a select party of guests. The rest of the fleet got under way without incident at 9.30 followed by the steam tug *Spindrift* crowded with spectators. The race was close. After 2 and a quarter hours *Wild Duck* was first round Lynn Well light to a salute from one of the light ship's guns and cheers from those on the *Spindrift*. Only four minutes behind was *Pearl*, owned by F.B. Archer of Lynn; the rest of the fleet rounded the light within the next ten minutes. On the homeward leg, *Wild Duck* was still leading at the Roger sand but ran aground on the west side of the Wisbech ridge, losing over ten minutes waiting for the tide to rise. The *Pearl* was first across the line at the Alexandra dock head in just under 5 and a half hours and took first place. *Wild Duck* finished third but was relegated to fourth place after allowing for tonnage.

Public servant

Frank was an alderman on the Town Council from 1851 until his resignation in 1874. He held a number of public offices, including chairman of the Buoys and Beacons Committee, Pilot Commissioner, and treasurer to several bodies, including the West Norfolk and Lynn Hospital, Lynn Savings Bank and Lynn Rifle Volunteers. In 1859 he helped to form the Lynn Rifle Volunteers, which he joined as a lieutenant. His brothers Samuel and Gerard were amongst the first to enrol. Frank became captain in December the following year when Colonel W. Swatman resigned. He was renowned for maintaining discipline and efficiency, which he did for seven years before he resigned the command in January 1867 in favour of Lieut Somerville Arthur Gurney.

Frank died in the early morning on Tuesday 19 September 1882. Three days later he was buried at North Runcton; his coffin was shrouded in his military cloak and his sword and his telescope lay on top. Eight bearers escorted the hearse, followed by a procession of seven carriages and over fifty fishermen. A public subscription raised money for his memorial and in 1885 a stone pulpit and reading desks were added to St John's church, known as the Poor Man's church.

Chapter 12
Form, Form, Riflemen Form!

Rallying cry

Invasion from France became a serious threat by the end of the 1850s and public concern mounted at the lack of military preparedness. The Regular Army had not fully recovered from its loss of the 20,000 or so men who had died, mostly from disease, in the Crimean War. Its resources were being stretched by the substantial reinforcements needed in India following the 1857 Mutiny. Almost every Militia regiment had been mobilised to take over the Regular Army's role in home defence. The cry went up to rebuild the volunteer units which had served so well at the time of the Napoleonic Wars fifty years earlier. In May 1859 the War Office sanctioned the formation of Volunteer Corps and, borne on a wave of patriotic fervour, a force of nearly 120,000 was raised within the space of a few months. The rallying cry was immortalised in Alfred, Lord Tennyson's poem *Riflemen Form!* Recruits were drawn predominantly from the professional, middle and artisan classes, preference being given to men who provided their own uniform and equipment.

Lynn Rifle Corps

Lynn was at the forefront. By the end of May 1859 a meeting of gentlemen, chaired by the Mayor, Walter Moyse, had decided to form the King's Lynn Rifle Corps. Within three months, nearly 70 volunteers had enrolled, of whom 40 provided their own equipment. Twelve gentlemen had promised to subscribe a total of £140 in cash. Messrs Goodwin & Co, Edward Lane Swatman, Daniel Gurney and John Sugars had each offered equipment for one volunteer. Colonel William Swatman of the 3rd Bengal Regiment of Europeans, who was on furlough at Lynn, and Frank Cresswell were appointed first and second in command respectively. The corps reached its full complement of around 100 by 1860 and was later known as the 5th, or Lynn, Company of Rifle Volunteers, part of the First Administrative Battalion of the Norfolk Volunteers. Frank Cresswell assumed command on the return of Colonel Swatman to India in December 1860. Josiah F. Reddie, from the renowned musical family, celebrated events by composing the *Rifleman's Polka*, which was published with a cover portrait of himself in his uniform as bugler of the Lynn Corps.

The uniform of the corps was grey with black braid, devoid of targets for enemy sharpshooters but not well suited to 'cutting a dash' with the ladies. The corps' band made its debut in May 1860, distinguished by a narrow strip of scarlet between two black braids on the trousers, small scarlet cuffs to the coats, and a scarlet plume in their caps. The *Lynn Advertiser* noted that the band's uniform was greatly admired and 'had in it just that amount of gaiety which was required to distinguish the equipment of the corps from that of a funeral procession'. The band's debut was on Queen Victoria's birthday in 1860. The corps had been invited to dinner at Ensign Somerville Gurney's home, Valley-field House, Middleton, five miles from Lynn. At half past 12 they assembled in the Tuesday Market place, where they were joined by parties of artillerymen, marines and other regiments who were recruiting in the town. The band played lively tunes as they led the march along High street, London and Hardwick roads, followed by crowds of spectators until they left the town behind them. Drenching showers greeted their arrival at Middleton, causing them to take shelter in the stables and coach house. The parade was postponed until a splendid dinner had been served in a marquee on the lawn.

The volunteers were typically in their twenties and thirties. James Fiddaman's close friends, James Bowker and J.K. Jarvis, both in their thirties, were amongst them. One of the first to enrol in 1859, and at 46 years the oldest in the corps, was William Monement. He gave his opinion on the ideal age for a volunteer one afternoon in August 1865, when, as Mayor, he entertained more than seventy members of the corps at his home at Reffley Spring. John J. Lowe of the Black Horse provided an excellent dinner which was followed by an abundant supply of 'Reffley punch' for the toasts. Captain Frank Cresswell thanked the Mayor for his hospitality and reminded him of his days as a private in the corps, especially the occasion of the dinner at Mr Gurney's when 'he was not carried out from the effects of the dinner, but from those of the efforts he had made in the light infantry.' The Mayor explained that he had resigned on the advice of his doctor, believing that 'When men got the wrong side of 50, very few were competent to go well through the duties of a volunteer. Those from 18 to 40 years of age were the effective men. There were exceptions, over 50, but he was not that exception.'

Parade, drill and rifle shooting

Regulations required that volunteer parades or drill should not exceed two hours and be no more frequent than twice a week in summer and once a fortnight in winter.

Volunteers were always enthusiastic about rifle shooting and particularly enjoyed contests. This need was recognised by the formation of the Norfolk Volunteer Service Association in 1862 under the presidency of the Lord Lieutenant with the objective of 'the promotion of rifle shooting and giving permanence to the Volunteer corps throughout the county.' Its first prize meeting was held on the Mousehold Range Norwich later that year. Sergeant Agger of the Lynn Corps, using an Enfield rifle, was one of the best marksmen in the battalion. At the Norfolk Volunteer Service Association meeting on the range at Mousehold in September 1865 he won the £10 first prize for the best score at three ranges. That year the Lynn Corps also competed for the Challenge Bugle, represented by Lieutenant Gurney, Sergeants Agger and Swatman, Corporal Elliott, and Privates Moyse and Haughton. They took third place and a prize of £3 against stiff opposition from 16 other companies.

Great review at Holkham

The first review at which all corps of the Norfolk Volunteers would parade was held on 12 September 1861 in the Earl of Leicester's Park at Holkham. The weather was magnificent. Major-General Sir Archdale Wilson, Bart, KCB was all set to take the salute at eleven o'clock. People thronged the roads from an early hour and began to arrive at the park soon after the gates opened at seven o'clock. Unfortunately Volunteers and spectators travelling by train were delayed for several hours while the Eastern Counties Company struggled to cope with technical difficulties, exacerbated by the unprecedented demand generated by cheap fares. The Lynn and Downham corps should have left on the first of two special trains at 6.45 a.m., picking up the Swaffham company en route. Their departure was delayed by half an hour and they were further delayed at Dereham because of an overheating axle on one of the carriages. They reached Wells at half past nine and marched the last few miles, arriving second only to the Norwich Mounted Rifles, who had left Norwich the day before and rested overnight at Fakenham. They took their place on the review ground at midday. The last to arrive were the Norwich and Yarmouth battalions whose train had left Yarmouth punctually at 6.30 a.m. but had been delayed by a failure of the telegraph between Dereham and Elmham. This stretch of line was single track, so they had been held for two hours until the regular train from Wells and Fakenham had reached Dereham.

Meanwhile, the visitors thronged Holkham Park enjoying the clear sky and brilliant sun and bringing splendid trade to the operators of refreshment booths: Mr Spicer of the Globe, Wells; Mrs Lack, the Victoria, Holkham; Mr Baker, the Three Tuns, Wells; and Mr Arnold, King's Arms, Wells. The volunteers were less fortunate, standing or lying in the hot sunshine on the parade ground, with only brief respite in the shade of trees or a visit to the refreshment booths. The Mayor of Lynn, Lewis Whincop Jarvis, and his wife were amongst the specially invited guests, members of the principal county families, clergy, and other dignitaries, who were entertained to a sumptuous luncheon and liberal refreshments in the mansion. By 2.15 p.m. all was ready and a crowd of more than 10,000 cheered the corps enthusiastically as 1,700 volunteers, including the Norwich Mounted Rifles and the Yarmouth Artillery marched past. Lewis Whincop Jarvis felt a glow of pride as the Lynn corps passed. It had been a tiring day for most of the troops but worse was to come as the railway company struggled with their return journey. The Norwich men did not reach their city until six o'clock the next morning!

Hunstanton encampments

Annual summer camps and reviews were always popular. Not only the occasion for the Volunteers to prove their readiness to an Inspecting Officer but also an opportunity to show off their skills to their wives, mothers, children, loved-ones and the public in general. They were seen as a good excuse for a holiday and, if it was at the seaside, many of the volunteers took their families to enjoy the air and the beach.

On Saturday 22 June 1867 the Norfolk Volunteers pitched their camp on high ground on the north-west side of the beautifully wooded park surrounding Hunstanton Hall, a fine mansion which had been inherited by Hamon LeStrange on the death of his father in 1862.

The atmosphere was a little subdued because the Prince of Wales had had to withdraw from a promised field day. An advance guard of drill sergeants and others under the direction of Capt Bathurst, the Adjutant, pitched ten lines of ten small round tents, thoughtfully provided by the government especially for the occasion. The site was surrounded on three sides by plantations and faced a parade ground which sloped gently into the valley. To the left were large tents for Lieutenant Colonel Duff, Majors Hollway and Boileau, and Capt Bathurst; to the right was the hospital tent. At the rear were tents for Quarter Master Wickes, police, press, canteens and stores. One tent, set apart from the rest, elegantly and tastefully fitted out, was for the ladies.

Volunteers began reporting on Monday morning. That evening Capt Bathurst reminded them all that they risked bringing ridicule upon themselves and the Volunteers if they missed this opportunity to improve their military skills. Roll call was at half-past eleven o'clock every night; all absentees would be reported by the Orderly Sergeants. Dismissal from the Corps was threatened if lights were not extinguished at midnight and perfect stillness maintained. Their duty done, the officers retired to Mr LeStrange's mansion, part of which he had placed at the disposal of the officers, including a dining room for the officers' mess, which was served by Fiddaman and Lowe. They dined and were entertained to music and songs by the 36 strong battalion band, under the leadership of Edward J. Gaul from Norwich. Their men came to terms with the rigours of outdoor life.

The Swaffham corps arrived on Tuesday morning, just in time to join the battalion for two hours of drilling. The exercise whetted appetites and the canteens of Wales and Henry Whiting (Golden Lion Hotel, Hunstanton), R. Spicer (Globe Hotel, Wells), and Fiddaman and Lowe were all extremely busy that lunch time. The troops relaxed in the afternoon, watching a series of impromptu boxing matches, until the bugle sounded for the Commanding Officers' parade. A large crowd of visitors encouraged them as they went through their paces for an hour or so. Lieut Colonel Duff pronounced himself particularly satisfied with the march past and complimented the band. That evening the East Dereham Volunteer Amateur Dramatic Company presented a succession of comic drama, songs, and farce in the Star Theatre, a large marquee erected near the Hall. The officers, their ladies and the rank and file volunteers greeted their performances with great laughter and thunderous applause. The music was provided by a small orchestra led by Mr. Bray of Lynn. There was a lot of fun in camp that night and no one was able to get much sleep. On this occasion a blind eye was turned to the breach of 'perfect stillness' required by Battalion Orders.

The sun shone brightly on Wednesday morning. That afternoon the battalion would be inspected, and over 10,000 visitors converged on the park by rail and road. By midday the canteens were doing a roaring trade. Visitors crowded around the parade square in search of good vantage points and were held back by volunteers on guard, assisted by Superintendent Rose of the Norfolk constabulary and some of his men. At half-past four o'clock, the 500 men of the Norfolk Volunteers marched into the square and formed ranks, their grey uniforms sombre against the brilliant colours of the ladies' dresses and the woodland greens of the park. The Inspecting Officer, Lieutenant Colonel Elliott, CB, entered spectacularly on a spirited grey horse and was received with a general salute. He took his position at the saluting flag and the admiring spectators cheered loudly as their townsmen marched past. Volleys reverberated from the surrounding hills as the corps showed off their rifle drills. The manoeuvres lasted nearly two hours. Lieut Col Elliott said that he would report favourably although they had performed rather under the average and put much of the blame on the officers.

The visitors began to make their way home and the disappointments of the inspection were soon forgotten as the men went back to their canteens. The officers retired to their mess, where they took solace in a most excellent dinner and wines served by Fiddaman and Lowe. Amongst the guests at the officers' mess was John Dyker Thew. Later that night the officers, their guests and several hundred of the men and visitors sang songs at a camp fire in a natural amphitheatre formed by a chalk pit. At eleven o'clock the National Anthem was sung; Colonel Duff asked the visitors to leave the park and commanded the volunteers to return to camp.

The Holt, Swaffham and part of the Dereham corps left on Thursday morning but the drills continued, visitors were entertained, a cricket match was organised in the afternoon, and the Lynn corps entertained in the Star Theatre that evening. More drills and athletic sports followed on the Friday and the camp was struck on Saturday. The venue was well-suited to the

Volunteers' needs and they returned in 1868 and 1869. Fiddaman and Lowe also returned, always prominent, serving visitors with luncheon and first class refreshments in their marquee.

Field kitchens

1869 saw the arrival of a threat to Fiddaman and Lowe's field kitchens. The officers of the Battalion had been encouraging the men to cater for themselves and that year the 23rd (Downham) company arrived with the 'Hunstanton camp kitchen', designed and manufactured by Frederick W. Abram, the honorary Quarter-Master. The apparatus was mounted on four wrought iron wheels and contained a hot plate, boiler, steamer, oven, gridiron, frying pan and two saucepans. The wheels and chimney were removable and could be packed inside the apparatus for ease of transport. It proved a complete success but James Fiddaman was still catering for the Volunteers in July 1878 when the 3rd and 4th Norfolk Rifle Volunteers held their camp at Yarmouth. On that occasion he was supported by Mr Steele of the Steam Packet hotel. Mrs Sharman of the Monument house supplied 'tea, coffee and other non-intoxicating liquids on Sunday to all volunteers in uniform'. James ran the officers' mess in the assembly rooms close to the camp, supplying liquid refreshment of a more invigorating character. His arrangements were judged comfortable, relaxing and highly acceptable to officers of all ranks.

Discipline

Lieutenant-Colonel Duff was so determined to keep a high level of discipline at Hunstanton in 1869 that each man was presented with a book of camp regulations and duties. He made immediate examples of Privates John Dasborough and Robert Waters of 17th Corps (Heacham) who had deserted their posts while on sentry duty. They were dismissed from the camp and threatened with dismissal from the corps; their misdemeanour and punishment were published on the notice boards that evening. On the following day, Captain John de C. Hamilton, the officer commanding the Heacham Corps, appealed for leniency on the grounds that they were both regular and attentive in performing their duties. Luckily they were allowed to rejoin camp but were required to perform extra guard duties.

Private Charles Colman of the Lynn Corps was less fortunate. He had been talking and making a noise in his tent after 'lights out' had been sounded. He was in no mood to be disciplined, perhaps because he had been taking refreshments in one of the canteens, which did not close until midnight. He was so disrespectful in the ensuing confrontation with the adjutant, Captain Henry Bathurst, that he was dismissed from camp and expelled from Hunstanton Park. Captain Somerville Arthur Gurney had no option but to dismiss him from the Lynn Corps.

Casualties

The Volunteers never saw action but their lives were not without danger. Just before nine o'clock in the evening on the first Sunday of the 1869 encampment at Hunstanton, news began spreading that several volunteers had been killed in an accident. Surgeon Thomas Masters Kendall and Honorary Assistant-Surgeon T.G. Wales junior were on the scene within half an hour. They found a large crowd of onlookers and soon saw that matters had been exaggerated. Mr Bull, a Hunstanton carrier, had been taking five volunteers from the Lynn and Holt corps into town when his horse unexpectedly swerved off the road - in the direction of the L'Estrange Arms - and the wagonette overturned. Mr Bull escaped without injury. The members of the Lynn corps got off lightly: Sergeant-Armourer Clarke was unhurt; Sergeant-Instructor Lorrimer had bruised his head; Corporal H. Green had wrenched his left side and spent the night at the Railway Hotel Hunstanton, before returning to Lynn the next day. The Holt Volunteers had fared less well. Sergeant-Instructor Leggett had broken his left leg near the ankle and, after it had been set by Surgeon Kendall, was sent to the West Norfolk and Lynn Hospital. Corporal Sooby had fractured the back of his head and was treated at the Camp hospital for several days. The incident was hailed as a success for the medical arrangements and the efficiency of the medical staff. The L'Estrange Arms had served admirably as a dressing station and been ideal for onlookers settling their nerves.

Chapter 13

Lynn Races revived

Spring races and rabbit coursing

When the organisers of Lynn Races decided not to hold the event in 1853, James Fiddaman seized his opportunity. He announced 'Lynn Spring Races and Rabbit Coursing' to be held on Thursday 10 February, featuring a race over one mile and a half with four flights of hurdles for a purse of not less than £5 added to a sweepstakes of 10s each. The Innkeepers' Stakes for 2 sovereigns, a sweepstakes for beaten horses and a trotting match for 5 sovereigns completed the card. Entries were required to be made at the Wheatsheaf inn by nine o'clock on the evening of Wednesday 9 February, when every horse had to be named, entrance paid and the rider's colours declared. Rabbit coursing broadened the appeal of the day's entertainment. James promised a good supply of wild rabbits, charged 3d admission for each dog brought on the ground and disallowed lurchers and greyhounds. Prize money was paid to the winners after dinner at the Wheatsheaf that night. James had proved himself worthy of a place on the organising committee if Lynn Races were ever to be revived.

Spurred on by the glories of Swaffham heath

While Lynn Races faltered and lapsed after a few years trial, the annual horse racing at Downham prospered. By the end of the 1850s the town had earned the title of sporting capital of West Norfolk. There was a well-fenced and well-kept course with an excellent grandstand at Crowe Hall Park, just south of Downham on the road to Denver, which was provided by George Wood who farmed the surrounding 700 acres. Thanks to the generosity of local gentry the organisers were able to offer stake money totalling around £100, thereby ensuring a good field for each race. For many years Mr J. Perring presented the Wood hall cup, a handsome silver trophy valued at £30. Race day was in July and was always a popular outing from Lynn and Wisbech. The many thousands who attended were as interested in enjoying the open air, eating, drinking and company as they were in following the sport. The first race came under starter's orders soon after midday but the card was sometimes unfinished by eight o'clock, when the excursion trains left for their return journeys.

The abandonment of horse racing at Lynn after 1854 was welcomed by those who found the links with betting and crime distasteful. It was regretted by many more, amongst them the sporting gentlemen who gathered regularly at Fiddaman's hotel to discuss the form and prospects at Newmarket, Epsom and local meetings. They would reminisce about the time when Lynn had had its own 'Derby day'. Self-confessed enthusiasts for the turf, they wanted the citizens, town and trade of Lynn to enjoy the benefits which the sport had brought to Downham.

The resurrection of horse racing on Swaffham heath in September 1861, after an absence of over twenty years, showed what could be achieved by an active committee of stewards and enthusiastic support from local gentry. Spurred on by this example, five gentlemen began meeting at Fiddaman's hotel in early 1862 to plan the revival of Lynn Races. Walter Moyse, Thomas Mawby and John Gamble had been closely involved in the attempt to establish Lynn Races ten years earlier. James Fiddaman, by now a moderately successful racehorse owner, gave them every encouragement. They were joined by William Henry Row, a Lincolnshire man, who became their honorary secretary.

Revival

Towards the end of August 1862 advertisements for King's Lynn Races began appearing in the *Lynn Advertiser*. Subscribers had given about £100 in stake money and trophies, enabling a programme of five races: the Lynn Corporation Handicap over 2 miles for £40, the West Norfolk Hunters' Stakes over 2 miles for £20, the Members' All Aged Selling Stakes over three quarters of a mile for £20, the Innkeepers' Plate of £12, and the Ladies' Plate of £6. Entries and stakes for the main events were requested to be received by William Row at Fiddaman's hotel before ten o'clock on the evening before the races.

At noon on Wednesday 10 September the rain clouds cleared, the sun broke through, and the course on the reclaimed bed of the old Ouse river at West Lynn began to dry out. Despite the refusal of the Great Eastern Railway Company to run excursion trains or to offer special fares, nearly 10,000 racegoers flocked to the course. Entrance cost pedestrians 1d, saddle horses 1s, horse and gig 1s 6d, four-wheel carriages 2s 6d and waggons 5s.

A fine grandstand had been built, beneath which was Fiddaman & Lowe's refreshment room. Alongside was a weighing room with the stewards' stand above. Immediately in front were the judge's stand, finishing posts and a stage on which the Lynn Rifle Corps and Saxhorn bands took turns to play throughout the day. On either side were booths and stalls offering amusements and refreshments. John and Mary danced a rustic polka on a makeshift stage of planks accompanied by a fiddle. A crowd jostled for the opportunity to throw sticks at Aunt Sally's blackened face. Beyond the rifle gallery, stalls were selling gingerbread and ginger-beer, fruit and lollipops, and oysters as big as cheese plates. Many of the well-to-do folk in carriages had brought their own supplies of pigeon pies, cold chicken, sherry and champagne. Everyone was in a holiday mood.

The races were well managed. Thomas Mawby and John Gamble were the stewards and William Row was starter. Thomas L. Reed, a respected Downham solicitor, was judge and Benjamin Calver, a Downham vet and shoeing smith, was clerk of the course; both had proved themselves at Downham Races. J. Perren of Newmarket was clerk of the scales.

At half past twelve o'clock precisely the runners in the Innkeepers' Plate came under starter's orders. Mr Weston's grey mare *Maid Marion* won the first heat and walked over in the second, delighting those who had taken advantage of the long odds which were on offer. The Lynn Corporation Handicap followed and was won by four lengths by Mr C. Rayner's *Court Martial*; James Fiddaman's three year old *Antonelli* had taken an early lead but ran off the course. James' run of bad luck continued when *Antonelli* was disqualified in the Members' All Aged Selling Stakes. His coloured mare *Nancy* came nowhere in the first heat of the Ladies' Plate, although she managed second place in the next; and his *Sugar Cane* was a poor third in a Handicap for £5. James' day had its compensations. Demand for the stewards' luncheon in the grandstand refreshment room had been so great that the 140 or so diners could only be accommodated at two sittings. And that night he hosted the stewards' dinner at Fiddaman's hotel, where the stakes were handed over to the winners.

Royal patronage

Emboldened by their success, the organisers decided to seek patronage from the newly-wed Prince of Wales, who had recently made his home at nearby Sandringham. It was a measure of the Prince's enthusiasm for the turf that he accepted, despite Queen Victoria's stern disapproval of the sport. The Mayor of Lynn, the Marquis of Aylesbury, Marquis of Townshend, Earl Derby, Earl Rosebery, Lord Stanley MP, Richard Bagge, Esq and several other distinguished gentlemen swiftly followed his lead and subscriptions soon totalled £400. Earl Westmoreland, Viscount St Vincent, George Bryan Esq and George Payne Esq were invited to be stewards. The stakes were quoted in sovereigns, the meeting was extended to two days, and three new races were added to the card: the Alexandra Stakes for two year olds over three quarters of a mile for a stake of £3 with £25 added to the prize money; the Prince of Wales' Handicap over three miles for a stake of £10 with £100 added if four horses started; and the Sandringham Park Nursery Handicap for a stake of £3 with £50 added if three horses started.

Thursday 3 September, the first day of the meeting, was blessed with delightful weather. The Mayor of Lynn had asked that the town's employers should make the day a holiday and crowds poured in from every direction by road, rail and river. Between 12,000 and 15,000 spectators enjoyed the occasion, bringing brisk business to the proprietors of the booths and stalls and to the bookmakers. The races were exciting, except for the Prince of Wales' Handicap where there had been only three entries so that no prize money was added and Mr H. Jones' *Eastern Princess* walked over to claim the sweepstakes. Friday's races provided excellent sport but showers threatened and the spectators were far fewer.

Amongst the spectators on both days were many children, playing truant for the afternoon. On the second afternoon, St Margaret's Boys school tried to entice their children away from the Races by treating them to a bun and a bottle of ginger beer each and allowing them to play in the Hospital field.

James Fiddaman had two most successful days as an owner. His *Reporter* ridden by C. Green took over £50 in prize money, winning the Hurdle Race on the first day at odds of 3 to 2 against and the West Norfolk Yeomanry Hurdle Race on the second day at odds of 6 to 4 on. Also on the second day, his brown pony *Nelly* won the pony race by three lengths to take the Silver

Cup, value £5, which had been given by Mr Willins. John Gamble was dismissive, claiming that his chestnut pony *Queen Bertha* could beat *Nelly* any day. James immediately challenged him to prove it, once round the Lynn race course, and backed his *Nelly* to win for £12 10s against 10s. On the day following the races *Nelly* made the running all the way and won easily by ten lengths!

The Prince of Wales did not renew his patronage in 1864 but the organisers were fortunate to keep the unwavering support of gentlemen such as W.A.T. Amhurst, Richard Bagge, and the MPs, Sir Wiliam Bagge and Rt Hon Lord Stanley. Coupled with the generosity of subscribers, this meant that Lynn Races could continue on the same grand scale as in 1863. William Row, their honorary secretary, had been overwhelmed by the workload so they appointed James Drake Digby as a paid secretary in 1864. Digby was a journalist in his late twenties, with a passion for sport, who became secretary to several other sporting events, including the Lynn and Hunstanton Regattas. He lived at 9 Buckingham terrace Lynn with his wife Amelia, son James and four daughters - Amelia, Eola, Katharine and Alexandra. In the early 1870s he set up as the proprietor of the cryptically titled Sandringham Intelligence Service, the headquarters of which were at 55 Rhadegund buildings in Cambridge.

Grandstand stakes

Behind the scenes an intriguing contest was being fought between James Fiddaman and John Haylock, the landlord of the Spread Eagle inn at Gaywood. The refreshment room in the grandstand was the prize. At the centre of all the serious sporting action, close to the weighing room, betting ring and finishing post, it was the natural choice for those seated in the grandstand. In 1863 James had had the concession, serving a champagne luncheon each day as well as the stewards' dinner at Fiddaman's hotel each evening. John Haylock had offered serious competition with a handsome spread in the Wisbech tent. John was an enterprising chap, a publican, who had won a government contract to deliver the mail, ran livery stables to service the mail coaches and, by the late 1860s, was claiming special appointment to the Prince of Wales. He realised that his trade was disadvantaged unless he won the concession in the grandstand. His chance came in 1864 when the old course was displaced by the Lynn and Sutton railway and a new course had to be constructed on pasture adjacent to the railway, close to West Lynn Railway station. The new circuit was about a mile and a quarter with a straight run in of about a quarter of a mile. A splendid new grandstand, with a bar and refreshment room, was built at the turn with a fine view up the finishing straight. John Haylock won the concession and James Fiddaman hired the Wisbech tent.

The meeting was on Thursday and Friday 21 and 22 July. The Great Eastern Railway offered return tickets to Lynn at single fares and ran special trains from Wisbech and Cambridge. The weather was fine and the crowds enjoyed good sport but attendance on both days was not so good as the previous year. John Haylock could not understand why his trade was so poor. He climbed into the grandstand, wondering why it was so empty. Admittedly James Fiddaman was serving the stewards' luncheon in the Wisbech tent but why was he doing such a brisk trade? Capt Machell's *Corinthian Tom* and Mr R.C. Naylor's *Tailor* rounded the last bend neck and neck in the Tradesmen's Optional Selling Stakes. Haylock watched as the horses galloped towards the grandstand and the finishing posts. From his vantage point it was impossible to see that *Corinthian Tom* was first past the post. The crowds alongside the finishing straight could see; and that was where James had pitched the Wisbech tent.

By September 1865, the grandstand had been moved to a better position alongside the finishing posts. James Fiddaman was back in its refreshment room serving in his usual superior style. John Haylock didn't get another chance until 1868 when James severed his connections with Lynn Races.

Pickpockets, welshers and burglars

The meeting in September 1866 was marred by several unpleasant incidents. Much of the blame was placed on the Great Eastern Railway Company which had run a cheap special train from London bringing down 'some of the veriest riff-raff of the metropolis'. Detectives from the railway police accompanied the train and assisted the local police on their arrival at Lynn.

At the start of the first day, townspeople crowded the betting ring, eager to back James Fiddaman's three year old *Begum* in the first race, the County Members' Plate. *Begum*, at odds of 4 to 1 on, won by a length and a half after a good race. Many of the bookies had insufficient cash to pay off the winning bets so early in the day. Fights broke out as they welshed on their deals and the disturbances provided an ideal distraction during which pickpockets relieved onlookers of their valuables. Amongst their targets were William Nurse of Friar's gate Lynn and Mr W.P. Wood of Middleton, both of whom lost gold watches. The crowd was so enraged that they embarked on 'a weeding process, - the sturdy Norfolk yeomen combining and clearing the commodious ring of these disreputable characters, to their evident discomfiture and mortification'. These men were lucky; it was not unknown for a frenzied mob of racegoers to lynch a welshing bookie.

Meanwhile other light fingers were at work in the town. Mrs Whitehead of St James's street was relieved of a sovereign and a shilling at her own front door by a stranger asking for directions. Mrs Woods of Gaywood was robbed of her purse and a gold ring while travelling by train from Hunstanton to Lynn. There was a richer haul at 8 St John's terrace, the home of Benjamin J. Whall, a clerk at Gurney's bank. While Whall was at work and his servants were at Hunstanton for the day, burglars entered through a kitchen widow and left with over thirty gold and silver items, including watches, chains, bracelets, ear-rings, brooches and rings. Whall discovered the loss when he returned home from work about five o'clock to find the house in disarray and jewellery boxes broken open. Mrs Platt's house in Exton's road was also broken into and a collection of gold and silver items were taken.

The reports of race day in the *Lynn Advertiser* were accompanied by a letter from 'Veritas', venturing the opinion that 'beyond a few public-houses, which are the resort of the betting fraternity, the business of the town during the races is not only not better, but is much worse than on ordinary days' and concluding 'I, for one, shall be glad if this week's races are the last'. The following week these sentiments were echoed in another letter which suggested that Lynn Races had received the 'coup de grace' and could be brought to an end if local gentlemen stopped subscribing. It was signed 'Lord Lyon', the horse famed for winning the triple - 2000 guineas, Derby and St Leger - that year.

J. Fiddaman begs to inform

Despite everyone's best efforts, the next few years saw a steady decline in both entries and attendance, often because of clashes with other meetings.

The organising committee lost its nerve after the bad publicity surrounding the races in 1866 and it was left to James Fiddaman to take sole responsibility in 1867. Thomas Mawby placed the course at James' disposal and the date was set for 19 September, the day after the great boat race on the Ouse between Sadler and Percy. Subscriptions raised nearly £300 in stake money, which was held by Messrs Verral of Lewes, and an excellent programme of races was arranged. The weather was fine, the Great Eastern and Midland Railway companies laid on excursion trains and the day's sport was enjoyed by many thousands of spectators. James had placed the betting boxes under the management of Messrs Valentine and Wright and no cases of welshing were reported. Richard Bagge was the only steward present. William Row was starter. Walter Moyse, John Gamble and James D. Digby were conspicuously absent.

The organising committee had regained their confidence by 1868 and set about planning a meeting for Wednesday 15 July. Their relationship with James Fiddaman was inevitably strained. James D. Digby had been most irritated when James Fiddaman had asked Messrs Verrals rather than himself to hold the stakes in 1867; he made it plain that he would hold them this year. The last straw came in early May when William Row declared that he would be both handicapper and judge. James Fiddaman immediately resigned from the committee and joined forces with John J. Low to organise a Grand Gala and Fête on Wednesday 8 July, just a week before the races. The squabbling culminated in a public exchange of acrimonious announcements in the *Lynn Advertiser* on 20 and 27 June. James Fiddaman begged to inform subscribers, owners and trainers that he was in no way connected with the races and nor did he have any transactions whatsoever with W.H. Row, or J. Digby. William Row responded by thanking James Fiddaman for publicly announcing that he was in no way connected with him. The races continued to be held for several more years but never matched the success of 1863 when the Prince of Wales had been patron.

'Always win at Lynn'

James and Jemima forged close friendships with the families of three men whom James had met through his interest in the turf. Two were owners whose horses always won at Lynn; the third was a groom in the service of the Prince of Wales. John Abel had been born at Ringland in 1803. A horse dealer and innkeeper at Norwich, he raced his horses regularly at Downham and Lynn throughout the 1850s and 1860s. He married Eliza, nearly thirty years younger than himself, after his first wife Fanny died. Eliza became a very dear friend of Jemima; around the turn of the century, both widowed, they lived together at Clapham Common in London. William Wolfe Goodwin was a Newmarket horse trainer whose sons, Thomas and Frederick, by his first wife Eliza, were both jockeys. William met James Fiddaman at Lynn Races in 1865 soon after his marriage to his second wife Lizzie. The Goodwins were frequent guests at Fiddaman's hotel and Jemima and Lizzie became great friends. A year later when Lizzie gave birth to a son, Weston LeCras later known as Wessey, James was proud to be his godfather. Before William's death in 1871, the Goodwins had three more children: Blanche, William Faulkner and Ella. Jemima kept in touch long after James' death in 1884, giving a wedding present to Blanche in 1891 on her marriage to Sam Pickering and attending Lizzie's funeral at Newmarket in 1903. Joseph W. Prince, born at Bath in 1836, represented the Prince of Wales' interests in 1863 when Lynn Races was under Royal patronage. He and his Irish wife Margaret became close friends of the Fiddamans and when their son, Joseph Edward Albert, was born in 1866 they asked James to be his godfather.

Chapter 14

Superintendent George Ware & the Borough Police

Lynn Borough Police

The Municipal Corporations Act of 1835 encouraged boroughs to set up police forces. Modelled on the Metropolitan Police, which had been established by Robert Peel in 1829, policing was to emphasise prevention with conspicuous patrolling by uniformed officers. The men were to be paid regular salaries and were not allowed to claim bounties for detection of crimes or recovery of stolen property.

The Lynn force was created in 1836 with the appointment of William Andrews as night superintendent and John Woods as day superintendent later that year. In February 1850, Newton Frederick Thornton, a Sporle man in his early forties, succeeded Supt Woods. Most of the officers whom he commanded were in their thirties and forties. The majority were born and bred at Lynn or nearby: William Andrews, Henry Blanchflower, John Carr, John S. Chase, Richard E. Cooper, Thomas Fulcher, Thomas Leader, Robert Softly, John Sutton and Henry Wright. Most of the rest were Norfolk men like William Andrews, Thomas Flegg, William Maud and James Tungate. Two came from further afield: James Gerrard, born at Hertford, and John Gerrard, born at Liverpool. Police duties were apparently no bar to other interests; Richard Cooper was a fishmonger in Norfolk street and John Gerrard a greengrocer in St James' road.

In Spring 1861 Lieutenant Cornelius W. Reeves, of the Royal Horse Artillery, succeeded as superintendent. The force had an establishment of three sergeants - Harry M. Butcher, John Carr and John Chase - and fifteen men, of whom four were river police. Supt Reeves was asked to resign in 1866 after he had been to investigate a charge of felony and had returned in a drunken state at four in the morning.

Meteoric rise

George Ware was born at Gibraltar in 1841, the son of a British Army corporal and an Irish mother. His father retired, the family returned to Hull, and

George went to sea on a whaling boat. He married Elizabeth when he was only 16 years old and joined the Metropolitan police a year later. After two years in London he moved to Leeds, where his aptitude for detective work was quickly recognised. One of his triumphs was the arrest of a father and son named Eagleton whose robberies had been plaguing the Midland railway at Leeds and Chesterfield. Both were sentenced to penal servitude. Within the space of five years George Ware had gained his sergeant's stripes, been promoted to inspector and by 1866 was deputy chief constable.

On Tuesday 4 September 1866 Lynn Watch Committee interviewed three candidates for the vacant post of superintendent. They unanimously selected George Ware against stiff opposition from Mr Berry of Yarmouth and Mr Pickering of Nottingham. They offered him a salary of £1 18s 6d per week, his uniform, residence in the house adjoining the Town Hall free of rent, rates and taxes, and an allowance of coals and gas. The Town Council accepted their recommendation that Mrs Ware should be appointed Hall keeper at £15 per year.

George Ware and Elizabeth took up their appointments at Michaelmas that year but tragedy was lying in wait. They had been at Lynn only a month when daughter Elizabeth died. Daughter Lilly was born the following year but survived barely twelve months. Elizabeth, wife and mother, was the next to be lost, leaving George to bring up John G. and Leon. George married again in 1870 to Rebecca Linford, a girl from Walpole, and had six more children: daughters Rebecca in 1872 and Rose in 1874; and sons Linford in 1876, George in 1877, Vernon in 1879 and Vivian in 1885. Tragedy continued to stalk his first family. In December 1879, Leon was only 17 when he drowned after falling from the yard arm of the barque *Virulam* in a storm off the Cape of Good Hope.

Watch committee omnipotent

Police forces were answerable to local government via watch committees, which sometimes kept close operational control over head constables. There should have been no political control but watch committees were appointed by, and often drawn from, elected town councillors, some of whom considered head constables as their borough's servants rather than independent officers of the crown. Some partiality in policing orders was inevitable.

Supt Ware had been in command for only six months when he heard that his force was to be inspected by Major-General Cartwright. He was keen to make a good impression so he asked the Watch Committee for permission to smarten up the police office and cells with a lick of paint and a splash of limewash.

George Ware
Courtesy of Norfolk Library and Information Service

The Watch Committee satisfied themselves that the work was necessary before authorising the Borough Treasurer to commission the work. On 24 June 1867 the Watch Committee looked on proudly as Supt Ware drilled his men. Major-General Cartwright went on to inspect the police office and cells before congratulating them on the efficiency of their establishment. He was particularly impressed by their arrangements for interim custody of prisoners and pleased to see that the men's pay had been increased since his last visit. He was less satisfied with their administration of relief to vagrants and directed that 'strict attention should be given to the searching of all suspected applicants, so as to distinguish as far as practicable the destitute wayfarer from the professional beggar and vagabond, and to regulate their relief and passes accordingly, and so classify them in the vagrant book'. Supt Ware was personally charged with relief of casual paupers; it was a post without salary which he found most distasteful.

On 9 July the Mayor, John Osborne Smetham, visited the police station to instruct Supt Ware that his men should use every means at their disposal to prevent public begging in the streets. Supt Ware resisted. He accepted that begging, hawking without a licence and obstruction were all offences in the eyes of the law but he had to think of the practicalities. He saw at first hand the hardships which people would endure in order to keep the family together beyond the harsh regime of the workhouse. He also knew that the reputation of his officers would suffer if they were reduced to chasing ragged, half-starved urchins from one street corner to the next with incessant cries of 'Move on, there!' The outcome of this frank exchange between the brash young superintendent and the middle-aged solicitor, who was Mayor and chief magistrate, was inevitable. Next day both men appeared before a hastily convened Watch Committee. John Gower Saunders was in the chair; George Holditch, John Dyker Thew and two others were present. The Mayor complained of Supt Ware's very improper and insulting behaviour. The Watch Committee found Supt Ware's explanation unsatisfactory and asked him to leave by Michaelmas. George Ware was dismayed at this outcome. His family had nowhere to go, he had yet to repay the money which he had borrowed for his move to Lynn and, in the circumstances, he would find it most difficult to find another job.

The Town Council met five days later, chaired by Alderman Saunders. Most of those present viewed the call for resignation as out of all proportion to the offence. They were appalled that the town should be losing such an efficient officer but had to accept that the Watch Committee was omnipotent in these matters. They were relieved when Councillor William Armes reported that the Mayor was willing to ask the Watch Committee to rescind the decision since Supt Ware had now offered him a full and satisfactory apology.

'One of the greatest coups in criminal history'

In June 1869 Supt Ware received intelligence that gangs of burglars and pickpockets would be travelling to Lynn on Wednesday 7 July to take advantage of the Prince of Wales' opening of the Alexandra dock. He assembled an elite squad to combat the threat: Detective Inspector John Shiels from York city; Detective Chief Inspector William Manton from Birmingham; John Moss, a detective sergeant from the city of London; Alexander Brown, detective officer from the city of Norwich; and Walter Fisher, a plain clothes sergeant in the service of the Great Eastern Railway Company. While the crowds flocked to catch a glimpse of the

Prince of Wales, detectives patrolled the town keeping a watch for known villains.

At lunch time on the great day, Henry Capstick entered the Crown inn near the South gates. George Rippengill, the landlord, served him with bread and cheese and bitter ale. William Dawson came in soon afterwards and chatted to Rippengill about Scarborough. He was soon joined by George Neville, for whom he bought ale, and both men joined Capstick in the parlour. There were only a dozen or so customers but the three men did not sit together, preferring instead to listen to the gossip. Dawson and Neville left after ten minutes; Capstick stayed only half an hour.

Most South Lynn residents had set out by two o'clock in order to claim a vantage point at the Alexandra dock. Mrs Pridgeon left 23 Valinger's road accompanied by her servant, Rebecca Newby, who took care to lock the doors and check that windows were closed. Robert Hall, who kept the Lincoln tavern on Mill fleet terrace, bolted the side and back doors and locked the front door as he left the house. At the Hulk in Bridge street, it was three o'clock before George Fyson, the landlord, managed to eject his last customer and set off to meet his wife at the dock. Deborah Nuccoll had been delayed, making alterations to a dress for one of her clients, and it was half past three before she left her lodgings at 8 Friars' street. Her landlord, Robert Brooks the master baker, his wife Eliza and their children had all left an hour or so earlier.

Opening of the Alexandra dock
Photograph courtesy of National Monuments Record Centre; copyright Phillips

The streets were deserted by three o'clock as Dawson entered the gate of 23 Valinger's road and used a skeleton key to open the front door. He signalled Neville to follow him into the house. They had reckoned without the eagle eyes and quick wits of Mary Billing, an elderly widow, who lived across the road at number 14. She had heard footsteps in the street and had peeped from behind the bedroom curtains. She had seen their every move. Followed by her daughter Phoebe Ann, she ran across the road to number 23 where she rang the bell and shouted 'There are robbers in this house'. Neville panicked and ran off towards the South gates. The Billings sent for the police. Their prompt action had saved Mrs Pridgeon's possessions and enabled the detectives to close the net.

The gang forced a door in the passage between Robert Brooks' baker's shop and the adjoining cottages. They ransacked every room in the house and broke open the till and cash box but took no more than £4 in silver and copper. Fortunately they did not discover the chest, hidden in an upstairs room, in which all the valuables were kept.

Soon after half past three, detective Alexander Brown saw Neville, Dawson and Capstick on the London road, talking together as they turned down Mill fleet and crossed over the bridge. Neville held back while the other two entered the Lincoln tavern. Brown waited five minutes before approaching the premises and trying the doors. Suddenly Capstick made a run for it over the bridge. There was no sign of Dawson. Brown summoned PC Abraham Miller from his post at the entrance to the Walks and left him to guard the tavern while he went in search of the culprits. He returned to the London road where he spotted Neville, out of breath from running, and immediately arrested him for loitering with intent.

About four o'clock Dawson and Capstick slipped into the yard of the Hulk. A ladder reached the back bedroom window; quick work with a chisel gained entry. They wrenched open a chest of drawers and literally struck gold: a large leather bag containing £4 4s in gold and silver, which was being held for a club; and a box containing two silver watches and a small leather bag with the Fyson's savings - £37 in gold coins.

Detectives Shiels, Manton and Moss had been keeping observation from a wagonette, driving around the back streets. When they reached the end of Bridge street near Whitefriars' gate, they spotted Capstick standing near the front door of the Hulk. Shiels seized and handcuffed him, while Manton and Moss searched his pockets but found only £8 or £9 in silver and copper. A few minutes later Dawson came up the lane from the Whitefriars' gate. Capstick shouted him a warning and he was off down Birdcage walk with Shiels and Manton in hot pursuit. Two passers-by tried to stop him. He pushed the first violently aside and gave the second a bloody nose. He knew that Shiels was gaining on him. As he entered South Everard street, he tried to dodge down a passage. He knew that the game was up. Before Shiels was upon him, he managed to throw away the silver watches, the large leather bag and the chisel. He fought hard but was overwhelmed when Manton joined the fray. A quick search of his pockets revealed ten skeleton keys and two picklocks wrapped in a handkerchief and a small leather bag containing £17 in gold. He was arrested.

Capstick and Dawson were taken back to the police station where a more careful search of Dawson revealed another £17 10s in gold, 11s 6d in silver, 3d in copper, a £5 bank note drawn on the Burslem and Potteries Bank, and a gold Geneva watch, gold guard and pin. That evening Shiels, Manton and Moss recovered the items which had been lobbed into the gardens at the end of the passage in South Everard street.

Twenty persons appeared at Lynn petty sessions during the following week. Capstick, Dawson and Neville were sent for trial at quarter sessions. Laurence Townley, George Hill and John Shaw were charged with intent to commit a felony and sentenced to two months hard labour at Norwich castle for being rogues and vagabonds. The remainder had committed minor offences. Jane Dye was charged by PC Abraham Miller with having stolen a Bradshaw's Railway Guide from the shop of Messrs Thew and Son. Notorious for being 'generally mad when she was sober and always drunk when she was sane', she was remanded in custody for medical examination before being committed to a lunatic asylum. Teenager John Rose and his pals, John and William Gent and John Weasenham, admitted wilful damage to a tree on the Public walks. They apologised and were dismissed with a caution.

Twelve year old James Reeve had appeared several times before the Bench and on this occasion stood accused of stealing 5s from the till of Henry Hobson, the baker in New Checker street. The magistrates were swayed by his father's promise that he would behave himself in future. They did not commit him for trial at quarter sessions but sentenced him to two months hard labour and to be once privately whipped.

Forty years later, in George Ware's obituary, the *Lynn Advertiser* recalled the events of the day as 'one of the greatest coups in criminal history'.

Guardian of public propriety

One Sunday in late May 1870, crowds were promenading up and down the Marine parade (South quay) enjoying the sights, sunshine and warm sea breeze. They were outraged when four members of the crew of a Dutch ketch, moored opposite the Mariners' Arms, stripped off and took a swim. The police were summoned and the men were arrested. Petro, Egberto, Lodwig and Julius spoke little English. Commander William H. Garland, vice consul for the Netherlands, represented them when they appeared at Lynn petty sessions the next day, charged by Supt Ware with indecently exposing themselves. He explained that they had not been aware that they were committing any breach of the laws of England, or they would not have acted in that manner. The magistrates could only deal with the case by sending the defendants to trial at the quarter sessions. They decided that such a course was too severe and discharged the men who promised not to repeat the offence.

Troubled with toothache

George Willey, an ex-soldier with five years service as a police officer at Lynn, was suffering from toothache as he patrolled his beat on a cold and miserable Monday night in November 1872. He eased his pain at intervals with a swig from the flask of rum which he carried. Just before midnight he entered the Mermaid and Fountain in Tower street where he had to remind Emma Flood, the landlord's wife, that it was nearly twelve o'clock. A gentleman standing at the bar offered him a drink, which he refused although he did accept a cigar.

About half past one outside Dr Reed's house in St Margaret's place he bumped into his old friend Robert Softly, a retired policeman. Ten minutes later he was in St Margaret's lane where he saw a shadowy figure at the door of Catherine Manning and her stepdaughter Honor Green. Both were widows, struggling to earn their livings as washerwomen. He called to ask whether all was well and they assured him that it was. By two o'clock he was in the High street, where he called on Arthur Bywater, staying five or six minutes to eat some bread and cheese and accepting his old friend's offer to top up his flask with rum. His toothache was much improved but he was feeling a little unsteady as he entered Tower street.

Just after half past two in the morning, George Black was one of the few people on the streets. An eighteen year old sweep boy employed by Robert Sainty, he was on his way to East Winch for a job, carrying a soot-sack and a machine brush over his shoulder. Sweeping still had a poor image despite the reform of 1840 which forbade the indenturing of child sweeps. Machine brushes were well-suited to the new and narrower domestic chimneys but a scrambling urchin was still best for a broad old-fashioned flue with awkward ledges and recesses. Not all sweeps were villains but sweeps were frequently involved in housebreaking. They had opportunities to see what might be worth stealing, reason to be out in the early hours before fires were rekindled, and climbing chimneys was ideal training for a cat-burglar. Society regarded them all with suspicion.

PC Willey confronted Black, challenging him to say which was the last chimney he had swept. Black claimed that he could not remember and seemed determined to provoke him by waving the sweeping machine in his face. Willey grabbed the machine and brandished it, causing Black to beat a hasty retreat, back to his master's house in Chapel street.

About three o'clock that morning, Sergeant John Barker was on duty at the corner of High street, close to the police office, quietly reflecting on his sixteen years of service as a police officer at Lynn. He was interrupted by an indignant Robert Sainty, accompanied by George Black, who complained angrily about PC Willey's behaviour and demanded the immediate return of their sweeping machine. Barker sent them to the office to make a formal complaint and went in search of Willey, who should have been at his rendezvous in front of Greyfriars Tower at twenty minutes to four o'clock. Barker waited a while but there was no sign of him. He began to search Willey's beat and eventually saw him in Regent street, reeling out of a passageway, leggings hanging over his boots, drunk and in no fit state for duty. Supt Ware's instructions were very clear in such circumstances; Barker asked Willey to return at once to the police office. Willey did not reply but walked with Barker along St James's street in the direction of the office. When they reached the Rummer inn corner, at the junction with Tower street, Willey refused to go any further. Suddenly he tripped Barker into the road, face first. Barker struggled to his feet and, in great pain from a broken rib, made his way back to the police office.

Sergeant James Tungate had been having a quiet night in the office until Robert Sainty and George Black stormed in to make their complaint. They soon left, Black for East Winch with another machine and Sainty to fetch his son for a job in the town. Barker staggered in about twenty minutes later and Sgt Tungate immediately summoned Edwin H. Woodward, the police surgeon, from his home in nearby St Margaret's place. No sooner had Woodward arrived to treat Barker than Robert Sainty returned in his cart, driven by his son John Robert, complaining that he had just seen PC Willey in a drunken state near Richard Nurse's jeweller's shop in St James's street. Sgt Tungate followed Sainty out of the office and saw Willey on the Saturday Market place. He called to him but his calls went unheeded.

Willey was confused. Why was Sgt Tungate arresting him? He reacted violently, knocking Tungate's helmet off before striking him on the head with his staff. He heard someone calling for Supt Ware; and then a little boy crying 'Oh Father! Oh Father!' He struggled in vain as Supt Ware and Sgt Tungate took him to the police office. He decided to make a last stand. No one was going to lock him up! He grabbed a walking stick from the wall and rushed for the door, striking out at PC Cornelius Gore and Sgt Tungate, whose face was crimson with blood from the wound on his forehead. Supt Ware eventually pacified Willey with a blow to the head with a staff.

PC George Willey appeared at Lynn petty sessions on Monday 25 November, charged with being drunk when on duty and with assaulting police sergeants Barker and Tungate. He was a popular policeman and the court was crowded with his supporters who had raised funds for his defence by a barrister,

Mr T.H. Naylor, recently elected Mayor of Cambridge. The magistrates were satisfied that Willey had been drunk and that the case of assault on Sgt Barker was proven. They took a dim view of Willey's behaviour and committed him to six months hard labour in Norwich Castle. The case of assault on Sgt Tungate was dropped. Willey was taken to Norwich that evening, disappointing the large crowd who gathered to see him off at the railway station next morning.

Chief Constable

The force grew steadily under Supt Ware, boasting an inspector, three sergeants and eighteen constables by 1879. In 1889, the Watch Committee accepted his recommendation that the head of the borough force should be designated as Chief Constable.

George Ware was suffering from chronic gout and attacks of bronchitis when he tendered his resignation on 2 May 1898, having completed forty years in the police service and leaving the Watch Committee four months within which to find a replacement. August was a busy month. On the 8th his son Linford, a Lynn coal merchant, married Katherine Elizabeth, the daughter of dock master Charles Bridges Clarke. On the 12th his police colleagues drilled in the Stone hall of the Town Hall before presenting him with a gold watch, bearing his initials on the case and an inscription inside. On the 15th at Lynn petty sessions he introduced his successor, Walter Granville Payne, to the magistrates before the Mayor gave him a testimonial signed by 142 subscribers and a cheque for £133 10s.

George Ware retired to Bournemouth where he died after a long and painful illness on 25 April 1911, survived by his third wife, two sons and one daughter. Vernon was living in South Africa, where he had served in the 1st Royal Dragoons during the war. Vivian was an architect in America.

Chapter 15

Lynn Regatta

Race around Lynn Well light

Weather permitting, Lynn Roads regatta was an annual happening in the 1850s and '60s. Sailing boats competed over a course from the port of Lynn, round Lynn Well lightship and back, a distance of forty or so miles. There were usually two classes, one for yachts and pleasure boats and the other for fishing boats belonging to Lynn, each with prize money of about £10 for the winning boat. Frank Cresswell regularly contested the first. The banks and quays were always lined with spectators to see the morning start, and even more crowded for the return many hours later, but only the favoured few could follow the race on board one of the steamers. Rowing increasingly drew the energy and enthusiasm of regatta organisers and the Roads regatta had lapsed by the end of the 1860s, although Frank Cresswell and friends attempted to revive it in 1872.

Lynn Great Sweepstakes, 1865

Once or twice a year, the Eau Brink cut was transformed into the Ouse championship course, 350 feet wide and perfectly straight for two miles. On Friday 18 August 1865 its banks were packed with thousands of spectators. Some had arrived on a large special train from London; many more had been encouraged by the Great Eastern Railway company's offer of return tickets at single fares. A large party of Tynesiders had been delayed when bad weather forced their steamer from Newcastle to put into port. The attraction was the widely publicised Lynn Great Sweepstakes, a sculling match over 3,300 yards between Robert Chambers and Robert Cooper, both of Newcastle, and the Londoner, Harry Kelley. Robert Chambers was reigning champion of the Tyne and had been champion of the Thames until Harry Kelley had vanquished him earlier that year. Each man had staked £50; £100 was to be added by the town of Lynn providing three came to the start. The winner would receive £200 and the second placed would save their stake. A good race was in prospect.

James D. Digby, secretary to the Regatta, was in overall charge of the arrangements. He was feeling very satisfied, having made an excellent profit on the Lynn Great Sweepstakes Distribution which he had promoted in partnership with James Fiddaman. This draw had no connection with the sculling match except the similarity of title, the coincidence in time and the benefit of shared publicity. Two thousand five hundred tickets had been sold at 1s each for a first prize of £35, second of £15, third of £7, ten prizes at £1, ten at 10s and thirty at 5s. The draw had been held at Fiddaman's hotel on the previous Wednesday evening.

All the concessions for entertainments and refreshments had been let and the banks of the cut were crowded with stalls and barrows doing a brisk trade. Here and there were the three-card tricksters, offering the foolish and unwary a chance to wager a sovereign on picking the king. The promised spectacle had drawn a good proportion of well-to-do folk in carriages, who made a beeline for the prominent Wisbech tent, where James Fiddaman was serving champagnes, clarets, sherries and brandies as well as sodas, lemonade and gingerade, all chilled with fashionable Wenham Lake ice. At three o'clock he served luncheon at 3s each to a large party, presided over by the Mayor, William Monement. Inevitably this gathering of the upper crust had also attracted the 'swell mob', well-dressed young men mingling inconspicuously, nimble fingers relieving many gentlemen of watches and wallets.

The minor races passed with little excitement. At nearly six o'clock it was time for the Lynn Great Sweepstakes. Kelley was 7 to 4 on favourite, rowing the same boat in which he had beaten Chambers, and drawn in the centre station. Chambers was 5 to 2 against, drawn in the west station. Cooper was 4 to 1 against, in a new boat built by Jewitt of Dunston, and drawn in the east station. The tide had just begun to ebb and the weather was fine, with only a light westerly breeze. The starter, Henry Everard, got them away after several false starts caused by the eagerness of both Tynesiders. Chambers was outclassed as a grand race developed between Cooper and Kelley. Cooper led the whole way and was a quarter of a length up at the winning post despite several valiant efforts by Kelley to pass him. Cooper's exhilaration was short-lived. The referee, E.D. Brickwood, water sports reporter for the *Field*, had closely followed the race in an eight-oared cutter, pulled by a picked crew of London watermen. Having had to give Cooper several warnings for taking Kelley's water, he decided to disqualify him and to award first place to Kelley and second to Chambers.

The stakes were presented at Fiddaman's hotel that evening. William Monement handed a cheque for £200 to Kelley but withheld second prize after Cooper's supporters protested that he should have been awarded it. Their protest was eventually disallowed.

Undercurrents

Letters to the *Lynn Advertiser* frequently criticised the Regatta committee for their paltry prizes and poor arrangements. It usually fell to James D. Digby, as secretary, to respond. In September 1866, he despatched criticism of the value of their prizes by observing that most of the competitors at the recent Lincoln Rowing Regatta had been 'gentlemen amateurs, who find the *honour of winning* a greater reward ... than the actual money value of the prizes given'. However, their arrangements were more difficult to defend, always a compromise between time and tide and forever hostage to the starter's lack of firmness or the competitors' lack of discipline. In 1866 the Cambridge University men had been late to the start in every one of their races.

In late April 1867 the Mayor, John Osborne Smetham, chaired the annual regatta meeting at the Town Hall. William Read Pridgeon, a local watchmaker, jeweller and photographer with a studio in the High street, proposed a committee comprising: John Osborne Smetham, William Monement, William Burkitt, Lewis Whincop Jarvis, Walter Moyse, J.K. Jarvis, James Bowker, W.W. Moyse, C. Miller, J.W. Barrett, James B. Rix, James Fiddaman, J. Horsley and himself. Everyone recognised the bias towards figureheads, whose business and other commitments left little time for the work of the regatta. J. Holmes and three other members of rowing clubs offered themselves as working members of the committee but were rejected on this occasion. John Smetham was reappointed treasurer. Thomas Franklin Cadman, printer and publisher of the *Lynn Record*, was re-elected as honorary secretary, while James D. Digby was confirmed as paid secretary.
James D. Digby and James Bowker were appointed trustees of the committee's property.

Despite these undercurrents, rowing was thriving at Lynn by 1867. James Bowker and Robinson Cruso laid the foundation stone for King's Lynn Boat House, which was to be the prestigious headquarters for Lynn Neptune and King's Lynn Rowing boat clubs. Lynn Alexandra club took to the water later that year. Spring and autumn rowing regattas were usual, the Prince of Wales was patron, and local nobility and gentry were generous subscribers.

Royal Regatta

The committee's determination to improve on the last year's arrangements was almost immediately thwarted when they had to settle for 31 May, the only day which suited the convenience of Cambridge University. High tide would be after five o'clock which meant that the first ten races, or heats of races, would be rowed up the river and spectators would see nothing but their start. In order to ease the waiting, seats were provided in an enclosure by the starting/winning post, admission by ticket only at 1s each.

James Fiddaman promoted his own rowing match in the week before the Royal Regatta. On the evening of Monday 20 May 1867, four-oared gigs competed over a mile and a half course up the Estuary Cut to finish at the Ferry landing. James Bowker was the starter and Thomas Cadman was the judge. The *Alexandra*, of Lynn Alexandra Club, was coxed by J. Holmes and crewed by Kerkham, Robinson, Rutter and Miller; the *Victory*, Lynn Rowing Club, was coxed by J. Barnes and crewed by Carey, Markham, Rust and Sampson; and the *Undine*, Neptune Boat Club, was coxed by C. Thurnell and crewed by M. Wilson, A. Goebbels, C.W. Harding and R. Howlett. The *Victory* took an early lead and held it until a quarter of a mile from home when *Undine* spurted and won by a quarter of a length. James Fiddaman presented cups to the victorious crew at his hotel on the following night, giving a sporting atmosphere to the serious business of auctioning riverbank sites for booths and stalls at the forthcoming regatta.

Friday 31 May was a fine day but attendance was down on 1866, despite the Midland and Great Eastern railway companies providing excursion trains. Thomas Cadman was judge and J.J. Ireland of London Rowing club was umpire. The first race began promptly but spectators could not see the finish and so missed the excitement. The racing was highly competitive, with first-class oarsmen from Cambridge, London and Newcastle-upon-Tyne vying for the titles and the trophies. It was the first visit by the London Rowing Club and their members performed exceptionally well. The Lynn clubs were outclassed but three of the ten races were specifically for Lynn amateurs and one of them, a gig race for the West Norfolk Prize of five handsome cups, was undoubtedly the best race of the day. The Neptune Club in *Undine* kept the oarsmen who had been victorious in Fiddaman's match ten days earlier, although now coxed by W.J. Freeman. Lynn Rowing Club turned out a fresh crew of G. Murrell, I. Rix, F. Jones, J.W. Brown and cox W. Churchman but were defeated yet again, this time by a length.

The great race of the day was expected to be the Championship of the Ouse for scullers, an open event which had attracted three northerners and two Londoners. The first heat had been won by James Taylor of Newcastle-upon-Tyne and the second by Thomas Hoare of Hammersmith. The spectators were excited by the prospect of a great final and even more so when it was announced that it would be the first race to be rowed down the river and to finish in their sight. Sadly they were disappointed. The two men had rowed no more than a quarter of a mile when Taylor put on a tremendous spurt in an attempt to draw ahead of Hoare. Unable to take the stress, Taylor's boat 'parted at midships, the two ends darting out of the water'. Taylor was left to be rescued while Hoare took the championship for the third time.

Ill-starred regatta dinner

Presentation of the prizes was planned for the Regatta Dinner in the Town Hall. Tickets, at £1 each including wine, had been advertised for several weeks and were available from James D. Digby, the offices of the *Advertiser* and the *Record*, and the bar of the Crown hotel. With only a week to go, so few had been sold that the committee reduced the price to half a guinea, failing to appreciate that this was still too expensive for many oarsmen, even if wine was included.

The Town Hall was beautifully decorated for the occasion and the regatta cups were proudly displayed. At seven o'clock everything was ready but the last race finished much later than had been planned and it was half past nine before the Mayor, John Smetham, eventually took the chair for dinner. Places had been set for 120 guests but only 35 were present. The committee was well-represented by Walter Moyse, William Monement, James D. Digby, William Pridgeon, J.W. Barrett, C. Miller, James Bowker and James Fiddaman, accompanied by his business partner, John J. Lowe. Mr Kent of *Bell's Life* and J.J. Ireland of London Rowing Club had been invited as guests of the committee. Men from the Cambridge and Lynn clubs were there to receive their prizes but members of the London Rowing Club were absent.

By ten thirty the waiters were beginning to clear tables in preparation for toasts and prize giving, when men from London Rowing Club began entering the hall. Amongst them were R.W. Willis, a member of the crew which had won the Prince of Wales' Prize, and Asplin, who had not competed that day. Brown, the porter at the door, had been instructed to charge 5s for entrance but his request was roughly refused. William Pridgeon, spurred on by James Bowker, jumped to his feet and spoke out before the latecomers could be seated, welcoming them in the hope that they would behave as gentlemen but doubting it in view of their language at the door. His outburst was drowned in hisses and uproar as the latecomers left the hall, closely followed by J.J. Ireland in protest at the insult to his fellow clubmen.

The Mayor was extremely embarrassed. He did not like to give the cold shoulder to strangers who had come such a distance to compete. He asked James Bowker and William Pridgeon to withdraw their comments. C. Miller proposed that they should be invited in to receive prizes; Walter Moyse offered to pay for their wine; and J.W. Barrett proposed an apology for requesting payment. All agreed and William Monement was despatched to reconcile matters. The men of London Rowing Club returned to welcoming cheers but not before they had forced William Pridgeon's departure. The Mayor apologised to them before completing the prize giving and toasts. It was nearly midnight, the party was in full swing and Walter Moyse had ensured a plentiful supply of wine. The Mayor left and J.J. Ireland was voted into the chair.

At two o'clock the next morning Supt Ware was next door preparing for bed. He had instructed Sgt Chase to lock up the Hall and turn off the gas after the party. He and his family had found their first few months at Lynn exhausting and he was looking forward to a good night's sleep. Suddenly there was pandemonium in the hall as a quarrel broke out between the watermen of Cambridge and those of London. Supt Ware went to investigate. He found J.J. Ireland standing on the table trying to restore order. The brief lull which followed his arrival gave Ireland an ideal excuse for going home and the waiters an opportunity to extinguish the gas light. Twenty or so guests, still squabbling, spilled out into the lobby and down the stairs into the street, where Supt Ware's exhortations to go home were met with chants of 'We won't go home till morning'.

Lights flickered on in the windows of nearby houses, shutters opened and curtains parted as annoyed residents watched the disturbance.

Sgt John Chase and PCs Edward Hains and Robert Seaman were on duty nearby, heard the commotion and rushed to the scene. They were just in time to see Supt Ware, in the midst of a mob, take the arm of Asplin and threaten to lock him up for breach of the peace if he didn't go home. At that moment James Fiddaman entered the fray to prevent the arrest and a scuffle ensued in which he punched Supt Ware in the face and was himself arrested. The partygoers, led by James' friends John J. Lowe and James Bowker, all the worse for drink, intervened to rescue Fiddaman. They escaped down High street but James Fiddaman soon realised his predicament and within ten minutes had returned to surrender at the police office.

Fiddaman in the dock

James Fiddaman's hearing at Lynn petty sessions was adjourned until the following Monday. His supporters turned out in force to hear the charge of assault which had been brought by Supt Ware. A dense crowd gathered around the Town Hall and, as soon as the door was opened, there was a noisy rush into the Justice-room. The crush was so great that the door could not be closed, which gave those unfortunate enough to be left outside an opportunity to catch a few words every now and then. James was clearly the favourite; Supt George Ware, the 26 year old newcomer, was not a popular man.

The case was heard before a full bench: the Mayor, John Smetham, and William Monement, William Burkitt, George Holditch, Joseph Cooper, Henry Bradfield Plowright and J.V. Hawkins, several of whom had been guests at the Regatta dinner. Other guests, including John J. Lowe, managed to get ringside seats for the contest.

Supt Ware, as the complainant, took the stand and described the happenings in and around the Town Hall on the fateful night. There was laughter as he described how he had been struck so violently on the mouth that he had fallen backwards against the wall. This was to be the first of many occasions on which the Mayor would call for silence and endeavour to restore order by threatening to clear the court. Sgt Chase and PCs Hains and Seaman were the other witnesses for the prosecution. Thomas Martin Wilkin presented James' defence. He argued that the events following the Regatta dinner were normally boisterous behaviour for gentlemen after an enjoyable night out - 'hallooing is not disturbing the peace'. If there had been any breach of the peace, it had been caused by the manner of Supt Ware's intervention:

> There is first of all your brave, calm, quiet, firm, gentlemanly superintendent of police, who, if he sees a few gentlemen retiring from a dinner party making a little noise, says 'My good fellows, go on;' and they would all give him a cheer, and home they would go. There is, on the other hand, your bumptious, cock-a-bobshy, quarrelsome person, who would give anything for a case, and anything for an opportunity of displaying his great powers before the magistrates.

He contended that Supt Ware had collared Fiddaman and provoked the assault, claiming that the police had colluded to tell a concocted story. Sgt John Chase took the stand. Middle-aged and on familiar terms with James Fiddaman for many years, he gave a robust performance in which he made it plain that James had been drinking heavily. PC Edward Hains followed and PC Robert Seaman, barely nineteen years old and only in the job six weeks, was the last to appear. Both were very nervous, glancing frequently at Supt Ware for support and guidance. All three men gave very similar versions of events but varying accounts of the foul language which had been used. James Bowker was the only defence witness. Unfortunately he could not convince the magistrates that he had been sober and had seen the assault.

The magistrates ordered the room to be cleared while they deliberated. Twenty minutes later the door was opened and a noisy crowd burst in to hear the verdict. The Mayor called for silence before announcing that the charge had been proved and warning James, and all those present, that they were determined to support the authority of the police. James was indignant, convinced that he had been collared by Supt Ware, but paid a fine of £2 19s 6d costs before leaving the court with troops of friends.

Postscripts

The London Rowing Club were undeterred and came back to compete at Lynn Regatta. James Fiddaman's involvement continued for several more years. In 1868, he and John J. Lowe unveiled their brand-new King's Lynn marquee which they claimed was 'one of the finest and best fitted up marquees in England'. It had been specially made for them and was 160 ft long although only 130 ft were used on this occasion. It dominated the other refreshment booths; its bar and luncheon room, with meals at 2s each, did a roaring trade. It also housed a committee room, where the trophies and medals were displayed.

One by one James' friends left the Regatta committee; J.K. Jarvis barely attended meetings in 1869 and James Bowker stepped down in 1870. Despite occasional difficulties, the regatta survived and was still going strong at the end of the century.

As the years went by, James Fiddaman and George Ware developed considerable respect for each other. When James died in 1884, he left George Ware the gold cameo ring which had been his fiftieth birthday present.

Detail from 'Sculling match for £250 between Kelly, Chambers and Cooper in the Eau Brink cut, King's Lynn'
The *Illustrated London News*, Supplement, August 26, 1865

Chapter 16

Lynn Gala

Athletic sports

James Fiddaman was excited when he heard about the athletics contests which were being held at Newcastle and Gateshead, where as many as ten thousand spectators would watch and bet on the outcomes. He remembered the popularity of the 'Rustic Sports' which had been organised by John J. Lowe to celebrate the wedding of the Prince of Wales in 1863. Why not promote athletics sports at Lynn? He planned his first meeting for Thursday 25 April 1867 but was defeated by atrocious weather. Undeterred, he postponed it to the following Monday, when a good crowd gathered at the Cricket Field off Austin street to be entertained between the heats of the races by the band of the Lynn Rifle Volunteers and Bennett, the champion arrow thrower.

About twenty young men had gathered from far and wide to compete in six races. James Fiddaman was the starter whilst James D. Digby combined the roles of secretary, judge, and, most crucially for those who wished to gamble on the results, handicapper. The partisan crowd had only one Lynn victory to celebrate, when Walter Foreshaw was awarded the Volunteer Cup for winning the 200 yards, open to members of the Lynn Corps only. They almost had a second when R. Gathergood reached the final of the Open One Hundred Yards Handicap, breasting the tape simultaneously with R. Mawby from Middleton but losing to him in the decider.

Petty squabbles

James Fiddaman made up his mind to create an event which would feature athletic sports but would provide an enjoyable outing for families. He outlined his ideas for a gala to John J. Lowe, who responded enthusiastically and offered to help with its organisation. In May 1868, James and John J. floated the idea of 'King's Lynn Grand Rifle Volunteer Gala and Athletic Fête' for early July, promising £100 in prizes and money to be competed for by members of the Volunteers and local athletic and football clubs. They gained patronage from the Mayor, Walter Moyse, and several other prominent local gentlemen, but their circular upset 'H.T.B.' His letter to the *Lynn Advertiser* complained that he was 'continually pestered with begging letters to subscribe to public charities and public amusements' and labelled the Gala a 'private commercial speculation.'.

A more serious confrontation was brewing with William Row and James D. Digby who were organising Lynn Races on Wednesday 15 July, just a week after the day chosen for Lynn Gala. They were incensed that James Fiddaman had issued circulars and taken advertisements to inform subscribers, owners and trainers that he was in no way connected with Lynn Races that year. The columns of the *Lynn Advertiser* became the battleground for a war of words which culminated in James Fiddaman being barred from the race course. Intentional or otherwise, this petty public squabbling generated intense interest in the Gala.

By the end of June, James and John J. had secured the Cricket Ground off Hardwick road, engaged bands, and booked artistes. They announced their 'Monster Gala & Fête', admission 1s each, 6d if purchased before the day, children of the King's Lynn Union admitted free. Four athletics events were planned: the Prince of Wales' Prize run over 400 yards for Norfolk Volunteers; the Alexandra Prize run over half a mile for gentlemen of Cambridge University; the Members of West Norfolk Prize run over one mile for gentlemen amateurs and members of athletic clubs; and the Borough Members' Prize for the pole vault, open to members of Norfolk football clubs. The entrance fee was 5s per event and each winner was promised a handsome silver cup, providing that six or more should enter the event and at least three should start. Competitors were warned that they would not be allowed to run unless they wore long drawers and Guernseys.

Almost perfect day

Wednesday 8 July dawned bright and clear. As James Fiddaman took Jemima and Frederick in his gig down Hardwick road towards the Cricket Ground he knew that it was going to be a scorcher. He turned off the road under an evergreen arch topped with flags, drove down the lane and entered the Cricket Ground beneath another beautifully decorated arch. The sight that greeted their eyes was perfect. Flags were fluttering from poles and festooned from tree to tree. John J. Lowe was already at work supervising the preparation of refreshments in their large new marquee, which was pitched on the south side of the field. Beyond, on the east side of the field, were a shooting gallery, an aunt sally and a carousel with horses driven by an engine which was puffing black smoke into the clear blue sky. On the north side were a large refreshment booth and three stages for the bands and other shows. Ethardo, the great spiral ascensionist of the Crystal Palace, Sydenham, was making the final adjustments to his apparatus, a forty foot high construction which bore a strong resemblance to a giant corkscrew. James left his horse and gig in the subscribers' private enclosure on the west side of the field and took Jemima on a tour of inspection. Frederick saw the three Lowe girls over by the carousel and went to investigate. They were fascinated by a group of local fishermen who were putting the finishing touches to their exhibition of one of the greatest curiosities ever seen, a monster of the deep, in fact a seal which they had recently captured on the sands in Lynn Roads.

James and John J. satisfied themselves that all was ready and at twelve o'clock precisely they opened the gates. At first there was only a trickle of spectators but by one o'clock this had turned into a steady stream, swelled by Lynn folk who had been allowed the afternoon as a holiday by many merchants and tradesmen. James breathed a sigh of relief when the bands of the Coldstream Guards and Cambridge University Rifle Corps arrived at half past one. Grand marches, waltzes and overtures breathed life into the occasion and the crowds continued to grow steadily as excursion trains arrived from Peterborough, Wisbech, Spalding, Holbeach and Long Sutton. Six or seven thousand people, amongst them many of the leading gentry of the neighbourhood, settled down to enjoy spectacular juggling by Professor Dugwar and aerial acrobatics by the 'far-famed' Danish brothers, Karl and Victor Lockhardt.

The crowd fell silent in anticipation when Ethardo appeared just after four o'clock. The great man was balancing on a ball which was about eighteen inches in diameter. He took a few unsteady steps, rolling the ball forwards and backwards. He moved jerkily towards the apparatus and began his renowned ascent up the twelve inch wide plank which coiled itself around like a corkscrew for one hundred and fifty feet to reach a height of forty feet. He had travelled no great distance when he slipped and the ball fell to the ground. His audience shrieked but he had landed safely on the plank. He returned to the ground, remounted the ball and recommenced his ascent. Five minutes later he reached the pinnacle, where he rested for a minute or two. He made the return journey backwards, taking another eight minutes and arriving to tumultuous applause and cheering.

The athletics were the only disappointment of the day. The foot races did not come off because there had been insufficient entries. There were only three competitors in the pole vault which was won by Mr Fellowes, who cleared nine feet, while J.W. Barrett took second place with a jump of seven feet six inches. That evening the Tuesday Market place was thronged with spectators to watch the ascent of a balloon, bathed in the glows from coloured flares. A brilliant display of fireworks provided the perfect end to a perfect day. The *Lynn Advertiser* reported that 'the fête surpassed anything of the kind ever before attempted at Lynn.' James Fiddaman and John J. Lowe had also had a most profitable day and thanked everyone who had helped by being 'at home' on the day after Lynn Races.

Proceeds to the West Norfolk and Lynn Hospital

The next year James and John J. moved the Gala to a more spacious field, alongside the Hardwick and West Winch roads at the Narrows. They decided to donate the proceeds to the West Norfolk and Lynn Hospital, hoping to deflect some of the controversy which had surrounded the previous year's event. Nearly thirty prominent local gentlemen, headed by the Mayor, John Thorley, offered their patronage. The programme boasted the return of the Coldstream Guards Band, supported by the Band of the Royal Artillery, Woolwich, and Mr W. Raymond King's Quadrille Band from Norwich. Mr Charles Roberts of Lambeth was retained to provide 'a grand company of London Star Artistes.' Athletic sports were abandoned in favour of a velocipede race, hoping to cash in on the great public interest which had been sparked the year before, in the Saint-Cloud Park, where James Moore had pedalled to victory in the first reported race.

On Wednesday 14 July the weather was beautiful. Several thousand people enjoyed the fairground attractions, band concerts and entertainments at Lynn's second Grand Gala. At about six o'clock the velocipede race was held on the West Winch road over a straight mile from the Sportsman public house at West Winch to the Hardwick corner. First and second prizes were a handsome silver cup and a gold pencil case. Nine gentlemen had each paid 5s entrance money but only eight lined up for the start. Amongst them was Robert Bullen, who was riding a machine built by himself and on which he had travelled the thirty miles from Fakenham that morning. The judge, Mr H. Bibby, checked that no one was gaining an unfair advantage by riding a machine with a leading wheel more than three feet six inches in diameter. Mr T. Oldham, starter and referee, followed the race in a gig. Bullen took an early lead, closely followed by two Lynn men, R.O. Birch and Edwin Bray. These three soon left the rest of the field behind. Near the half way point Birch had a close encounter with an oncoming pony and trap which forced him on to the footpath but he quickly recovered. Crowds lined the route to the finish, shouting encouragement and cheering as Bullen crossed the line in two minutes and forty five seconds. Birch was 15 yards behind in second place and Bray came in third. Robert Bullen waited for the prize giving before mounting his bicycle for the thirty mile return to Fakenham.

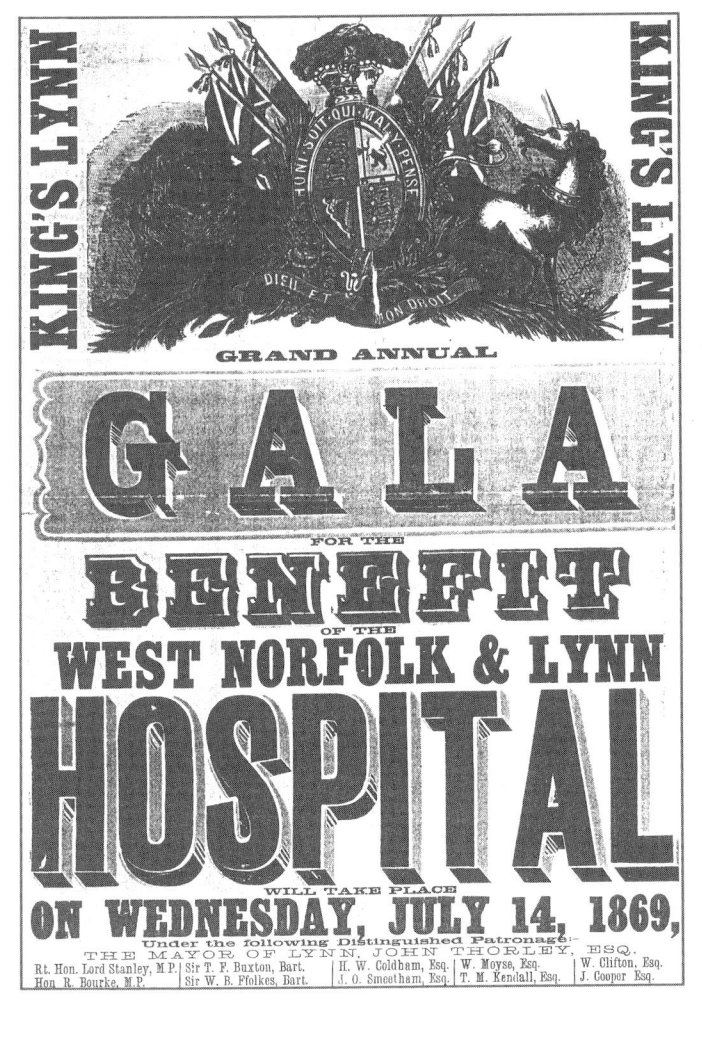

The day ended with dancing and fireworks. There had been something for everyone to enjoy. The Gala had made a good profit enabling James and John J. to send a cheque for £35 to S.M.W. Wilson, house surgeon and secretary to West Norfolk and Lynn Hospital. Fiddaman & Lowe had also made a good profit catering tactfully for the refreshment needs of all classes and tastes. James and John J. vowed to make the Gala an annual event for the benefit of the hospital.

Poster advertising the first Lynn Gala in aid of West Norfolk & Lynn Hospital
Courtesy of King's Lynn Museums

Bank holidays

In 1871 bank workers were guaranteed holidays on Easter Monday, Whit Monday, the first Monday in August and Boxing Day. This entitlement was extended to many public servants in 1875 and most workers were enjoying these annual holidays within a decade. King's Lynn was at the forefront when it came to the informal adoption of these arrangements. In 1872 John Dyker Thew, as Mayor, called upon the merchants, solicitors and tradesmen of Lynn to keep Whit Monday as a general holiday throughout the town and gave his patronage along with other prominent gentlemen to the 'Athletic Sports and Pony Races' which were being organised for that day by James Fiddaman and John J. Lowe. Within a week nearly 150 employers had agreed to observe all four days as general holidays and placed a signed undertaking to that effect in the *Lynn Advertiser* of 11 May.

Whit Monday, 20 May 1872, saw a bright sunrise as dull, wet and cold weather cleared miraculously. Seven hundred Lynn folk took excursion trains to Hunstanton to enjoy a few hours at the seaside. Captain John Hillman Howard took sixty trippers to the cockle sands on the steam tug *Spindrift* in the morning and nearly two hundred to Lynn Roads in the afternoon. The athletic sports and pony races were far and away the biggest attraction, drawing between three and four thousand spectators to the old cricket ground near Hardwick bridge which had been lent for the day by Messrs Eyre & Co. The band of the 6th Cambridgeshire Militia entertained the crowds throughout the afternoon and evening. James Fiddaman was disappointed when his *Rob Roy* was beaten in the one mile race for ponies but otherwise the day had been most profitable.

James and John J. scheduled their Grand Annual Gala for Monday 5 August 1872. Despite a dull morning, steady rain by noon and a heavy thunderstorm that night, people were in a holiday mood. Hunstanton attracted over three thousand day trippers: nearly a thousand on a special train from London, half as many again from Lynn, and several hundreds each on the steamers *Spindrift* from Wisbech and *Cumbrian* from Boston. The *Spindrift* was wrecked in the storm that night, fortunately not before she had returned her trippers safely to Wisbech. The Gala was once again the principal attraction at Lynn, drawing over one thousand spectators, who enjoyed the band of the Coldstream Guards, fairground attractions and a 'Grand Congress of Comicalities' provided by the Brothers Nemo of Westminster and their troupe. The weather brought the proceedings to a premature close in the evening and the fireworks had to be postponed.

Taking a back seat

James Fiddaman enjoyed reasonably robust health until 1873, when he was overtaken by one of the hazards of his occupation and suffered severely from a stomach ulcer. Several times in the years which followed, he reluctantly left his business, for weeks or even months at a time, visiting various resorts in Great Britain and on the continent in the hope that the change of air might improve his condition. He was no longer able to guarantee his personal attention for the prolonged periods required to organise a big event such as the Gala.

William Wardale of the Royal Standard inn, County Court road, who had taken over the Gala by August 1874, faced different threats. The railways had been a boon in the early years, bringing trippers from far and wide to enjoy Lynn Races, Regatta and Gala. However, better off Lynn folk were quick to take advantage of this cheap form of travel to spend bank holidays away from the town. Gala attendance declined and the middle classes became less well represented. Wardale stuck to the well tried formula of military band, circus and music hall acts, and athletic or vocal contests for local amateurs, concluding with a display of fireworks. He was not pleased with the Whit Monday Gala in 1876, when the weather was wet, attendance was well down on previous years, and the *Lynn Advertiser* observed that 'a large proportion of the assemblage may be said to have been of that class whose company is not much desired by the more respectable of the population.'

In 1877 there was a clash of events on Whit Monday. Stoodley & Harmston, whose New Grand Continental Circus was installed on the Tuesday Market place, had organised a Grand Fête and Gala at the Old Cricket Field. It started with a procession from the Circus at one o'clock, led by a military band. Omnibuses were run to and from the fête for a fare of 4d by Samuel Marshall of the Globe and James Reeder of the Woolpack. Further out of town, in a field adjoining Hardwick Narrows, Mr Pollard of the Crown hotel was holding King's Lynn Athletic Sports for the benefit of West Norfolk and Lynn Hospital. This event was patronised by the Mayor, John Dyker Thew, and was in aid of a good cause but Stoodley & Harmston's fête proved the bigger draw. The sports made a loss while the Hospital fund benefited by

3 guineas thanks only to Pollard's personal donation. On this occasion, James Fiddaman had invested his energies in refreshments at the fête and was amply rewarded.

James Fiddaman returned to a more prominent role in 1878. He brought together many of his closest friends, including William Murrell the Norfolk street hairdresser, to organise the West Norfolk Royal Athletic Sports for amateurs only. The committee for this Second Annual Festival under the patronage of the Prince of Wales was dominated by High street tradesmen: Robert Goodwin the grocer, John Henry Noakes the boot maker, Joseph C. Potter the tobacconist, William King the watchmaker and jeweller, and Isaac Rix the haberdasher. The sports were held on Whit Monday afternoon in Fiddaman's field off the Gaywood road which had been converted into an athletics ground by staking out a quarter mile track and constructing a grandstand near the winning post. The arrangements would not have been complete without a bandstand and large marquees for refreshments. The event was a big attraction, drawing more than three thousand spectators who enjoyed keen contests in a dozen races and only once had to shelter from heavy rain. James stepped into the breach for a second time later that year when he improvised an August bank holiday gala on his 'athletics ground' on the Gaywood road. A good crowd enjoyed the usual entertainments and races, including a two mile open amateur handicap bicycle race with a first prize of 2 guineas which was won by F. Warnes of Terrington Marsh on one of Plowright's patent machines. The champion boy walker, 13 year old William Cooke, was challenged to walk 3 miles in 30 minutes. The time was well within his capability but he failed by six seconds. Those who had placed wagers on the outcome may not have been entirely satisfied with his explanation that he was unused to walking on grass and had been uncomfortable with the spikes in his shoes!

James continued to promote fêtes and galas but increasingly took a back seat. He relied on travelling shows to provide the entertainment and organise the competitions as in October 1879, when Mr J. Lifely 'the well-known Star Auctioneer of all now travelling' announced his 'Grand Monstre Fête and Gala in a field known as the "Athletic Grounds", kindly lent by Mr Fiddaman, five minutes walk from railway station.' The Gala in one form or another continued to be a feature of bank holiday life at Lynn into the twentieth century.

Chapter 17

Frederick Fiddaman

In September 1876 Frederick set out to see the world. He went to London where he signed articles for nine months as an engineer's steward on the *Ionia*, a London registered steamer, captained by Charles Hyde. His first voyage would be to Alexandria in Egypt and then via the Black Sea into the Sea of Asof to the Russian port of Rostov. The *Ionia* was an iron screw steamer, just over three hundred feet long with a displacement of nearly 1,800 tons, which had been built at Shields in 1856.

The *Ionia* left the Tyne on 24 September and passed Dover two days later. She was expected at Alexandria within two weeks but the days passed without news and the seamen's families grew increasingly concerned for the safety of their loved ones. Shipmasters who had crossed the Bay of Biscay towards the end of September told of the worst storms that they had ever encountered and several steamers had come to grief. The *Zampa*, of Newcastle, bound for Port Said was also missing in the area. About 17 October wreckage was picked up and taken into St. Michael's Mount: a vessel's royal yard, 36 ft in length, and a fore hatch, 10 ft in length. More wreckage was washed ashore at Land's End, consisting of planks, an iron beam 15 and a half ft in length, and a life buoy, painted white, and marked 'Ionia,... London'.

James' and Jemima's worst fears were confirmed by *The Times* on Monday 30 October 1876:

> It is feared that the missing steamer Ionia has been lost. For a steamer that left Tyne on the 24th September last, passed Dover on the 26th, and is now three weeks overdue at Alexandria, something more than ordinary anxiety may be entertained, as to her safety...... As to the crew, there is a faint possibility of their having been picked up by some outward-bound vessel, in which case we may not hear of them for another four or five months...... The following telegram was received yesterday relating to the Ionia:- 'From vestiges found or washed ashore, no hope remains.' We understand that

reinsurances were effected on the vessel some days since at 80 guineas.

They knew that they were clutching at straws but hoped against hope that Frederick might have been rescued from the shipwreck and would return to Lynn. There were no survivors; twenty eight men were lost. The motto which James had adopted for his trade mark, 'Never venture out of your depth until you are able to swim', was to be a cruel and constant reminder of his son's fate.

Chapter 18

Frederick Savage

Hard times

Frederick Savage was born at Hevingham, near Aylsham, on 3 March 1828, the eldest son of William and Susannah Savage. Both parents were hand-loom weavers, industrious but fallen upon hard times as their cottage industry suffered from trade recessions and the introduction of mechanisation. William had to sell his farm and cottages to the local squire and took to poaching in order to feed the family. One night he and his companions threatened a gamekeeper. They were arrested, tried and sentenced to fourteen years penal servitude. William was deported to Tasmania but was released after seven years. His family declined to join him and he lived his remaining years alone on the other side of the world. Susannah died at Hevingham in October 1896 aged 89.

Formative years

Frederick had little chance of education at the Church Sunday school and village free school. He began work at the age of ten, preparing wood for a hurdle maker, Mr Dye, on Robert Marsham's estate at Stratton Strawless. He worked for a succession of masters at Dereham, Gressenhall and Dillington, learning how to work iron and make agricultural implements. In 1850 he was working for Holmes & Sons at their Prospect Works, Norwich, when he fell in love with Susannah Bloyce, who lived at Tuttington ten miles to the north. They married at Norwich on 26 August that year.

Frederick moved to Lynn in 1851, as foreman in charge of woodwork, making steam threshing machines in Charles Willett's workshop in Baker lane. Soon he was confident enough to go into business on his own, with a forge in the Mermaid and Fountain yard in Tower street, making iron and wood rakes. A year later he was in roomier premises in Railway road, making implements as diverse as seed drills and threshing machines.

The tower of St. James' workhouse collapsed on the morning of Sunday 20 August 1854, killing Mr Andrews, who was in the tower repairing the clock.

Miraculously only one other person was killed although two more were buried alive. Two years later a much larger workhouse had been built on new land and Frederick moved his works to the derelict St James site, having purchased it in partnership with Richard Munson, a farmer from Walpole St Peter. Here he built a traction engine for James Walker of Terrington St. Clement; called *The Juggernaut*, it was the first to be seen on public roads around Lynn.

Apprentices at St Nicholas' Works

Business prospered. In 1860 Frederick parted company with Richard Munson and established St Nicholas' Works in premises in St Nicholas street which he rented from William Armes. He relied on his foremen to maintain discipline in the works, employing two brothers, Joseph and Robert Bunting, the first of whom he had met when both had worked for Charles Willett. He held them in the highest regard but suspected that they were too easygoing. Matters came to a head in 1872. Charles Maltby had been an apprentice for nearly three and a half years and was paid 8s per week. He was one of several lads whose behaviour was disruptive and was renowned for being cheeky to the foremen. Twice on the morning of Tuesday 16 July, Robert Bunting caught him away from his lathe, straightening iron on the other side of the works. On the second occasion he told Maltby that he would stop his time and that he should see Mr Savage before returning to work. Maltby returned to the works two days later without having seen him. Frederick decided to make an example of him and took Maltby before the magistrates at Lynn petty sessions on 22 July, charged with being disobedient and absent from his work without cause or excuse. The magistrates dismissed the case when Maltby accepted Frederick's offer to return him to work if he would promise to obey the foremen. Maltby had to pay the expenses of 5s.

St Nicholas' Ironworks

In the early 1870s Frederick purchased several acres of land on the east side of the old river Ouse, nearby the Alexandra dock, and built the new St Nicholas' Ironworks. There were an iron and brass foundry, forges, warehouses, well-equipped workshops, offices, and his own residence, Estuary House. By 1878 he was selling a patent cultivating system, of his own design and manufacture, which was powered by a ten horse power traction engine, called *Agriculturist*, complete with self-moving anchors, and a self-lifting and self-turning cultivator.

Around 1880 Frederick began to create fairground rides. His 'circular velocipede' - 24 bicycles linked to each other, running on a circular track, and pedalled by the riders - was soon superseded by a steam powered version with 48 seats. Thereafter he patented many rides, some of whose names convey quite neatly the sensations they induced: 'Sea on land', 'Galloping horses', and 'The circular switchback'. His truck with engine and gear for driving fairground machines proved extremely popular and was exported world-wide.

Frederick was a paternalistic employer as shown at his daughter Sarah's marriage to Francis Smith, the Midland railway station master, on Thursday 17 January 1878. The ceremony was at St. Nicholas' chapel late that morning, followed by an afternoon breakfast for the wedding party at Estuary House, before the happy couple left for London on the evening train. That same afternoon about 130 workmen sat down to a substantial dinner, served by John J. Lowe in one of the workshops, and followed by enthusiastic toasts and singing. Amongst the wedding gifts were a very elegant silver-plated tea and coffee service and butter cooler presented by the employees.

A Savage ploughing machine
Courtesy of King's Lynn Museums

Public life

Frederick Savage began his active support for the Conservative party around 1868. That was the year when he and rival Alfred Dodman attended the annual dinner of the Lynn Loyal and Constitutional Association in the Athenaeum, where James Fiddaman served an excellent meal to about

400 guests. It was not until 1883 that Frederick was elected to the Town Council to represent North Ward, following the resignation of Richard Bagge. He held the seat for ten years before being elected an alderman. He was chosen Mayor in 1889, at a time when the West Norfolk and Lynn hospital was nearly £1000 in debt and it was largely due to his efforts and personal generosity that the debt was cleared. His friends celebrated his magnificent achievements as Mayor by collecting several hundred pounds, including about £9 in penny contributions from over 2,000 poorer citizens of Lynn, and erecting his statue on London road, near the South Gates.

While holidaying in Amiens in midsummer 1894, Frederick was drenched in a sudden and severe thunderstorm. His already poor health was further aggravated on the journey home, when he had to endure a night crossing from Dieppe to Newhaven on board a steamship without sleeping accommodation. He never quite recovered from this episode, although he continued to play an active role in business and public affairs. He died on the morning of Tuesday 27 April 1897 and was buried at Hardwick road cemetery, where his children erected a large monument to his memory.

Chapter 19

Alfred Dodman

From Titchwell to Lincoln

Alfred Dodman was born on 14 September 1833 at Thornham, one of several children by the first marriage of Martin Dodman, a wealthy maltster, ship owner, and farmer of 800 acres. Alfred's elder brother, Martin, a confirmed bachelor, took over the running of the farm at Titchwell and gained quite a reputation with the local butchers for his shorthorn cattle. His father's second marriage was to Eliza, a Docking girl young enough to be his daughter, by whom he had three sons: Arthur, Augustine and Henry.

Alfred began work as an apprentice to Messrs Clayton and Shuttleworth, the Lincoln engineers. It was here that he met and married Mary Slator. They moved to Lynn in 1852 and were later followed by Mary's brother, John W. Slator, who was in business in the 1880s as an agricultural implement maker, employing two men and a boy.

Business at Lynn

Alfred set up a small business as an iron founder and engineer in Austin street but soon outgrew the premises. By 1855 he had entered into a seven year lease with Charles Willett for his works off Baker lane, where Frederick Savage had been employed just a few years earlier. Alfred's Baker Lane Foundry thrived on repair work, especially his promise to supply at short notice all those critical items, such as gutta-percha driving bands, gauge glasses and India rubber rings, which cost operators so dearly while their engines were out of use. By 1864 Alfred had established his St James' engineering works on a site at the back of the County Court which had formerly been occupied by the old workhouse and been used for a time by Frederick Savage. He sold an 'assortment of Agricultural Implements, consisting of Steam Engines, Thrashing Machines, Straw Elevators, Grinding Mills, Corn Screens and Dressing Machines, Saws, Benches, Chaff Cutters, Pulpers, Cake Breakers and every other requisite for the farm'.

Alfred's engineering interests extended beyond agricultural implements. In 1867 Hunstanton was improving its attractions for summer visitors. Sam Dunn's embrace as he helped ladies ashore from pleasure boats had proved such a deterrent that a landing stage was installed. Mr True, previously a railway guard, introduced donkey rides and the Lynn and Hunstanton Bathing Saloon Company was adding to its fleet of bathing machines. Alfred Dodman supplied the new machines, which incorporated ingenious spring-drawbars to prevent ladies being thrown off-balance by the usual jerk at the first pull of the horse. They were spacious, comfortable and equipped with 'every requisite, including bathing dresses of an improved description'.

His business outgrew the St James's works and in 1875 he constructed the Highgate Ironworks on one acre of land off Gaywood road alongside Highgate bridge and the railway to the Alexandra Dock. Here he continued to develop and build a wide range of innovative machines for farmers and industrialists. Amongst his products were traction engines, which he sold in keen competition with Frederick Savage.

Newfangled machines

Traction engines frightened horses. Agricultural labourers saw steam powered machines as a threat to their livelihood. The newfangled machines were treated with suspicion. They were also hazardous to make and accidents were common. One morning in February 1867 at Alfred's Engine Works, St James' end, some men were welding up a large tyre for the wheel of a threshing engine. The component, weighing about 300 pounds, slipped off the anvil. It fell on the leg of Robert Bone, an eighteen year old apprentice, breaking it below the knee. He was taken to hospital and thankfully recovered from the incident.

Using the machines could be even more hazardous. In August 1880, one of Alfred's employees, a man called Ollett, was in charge of a traction engine at Hillington when he caught one of his hands in the driving wheel and crushed it, although not seriously! Nineteen year old Thomas Riches was less fortunate. One Friday in September 1869, he was threshing corn for Mr Clifton at West Lynn, working with Martin Farmer and William Rose on a machine owned by Mr Crowe of Gaywood. Riches and Farmer were on the corn stack and Rose was feeding the machine. About midday it came on to rain heavily. Rose slowed the machine to get his waistcoat. Riches followed closely behind Farmer as they came off the stack. He lost his footing and slipped into the machine which ground to a halt. Mr Clifton heard the cries for help and was soon on the scene. Rose had to dismantle the machine in order to release Riches, whose leg was badly crushed and bleeding profusely. They took him to West Norfolk and Lynn Hospital where he was soon attended by the house surgeon, Stevenson Morton Wilson. He had lost so much blood that he died early the following morning.

Tireless worker

Alfred was a staunch Conservative and a Churchman who took a keen interest in the affairs of the town. He was elected to the Town Council as representative of South Ward in 1874 and was returned continuously until he retired in 1889. He served on many public bodies: Board of Guardians for twenty years; Paving Commission until its abolition in 1877; Norfolk Court of Sewers; River Ouse Haling Commission; and Lynn Municipal Charity Trustees. He was also a King's Lynn Income Tax Commissioner, Chairman of the first district Ouse Bank Commissioners, and well known as a county and Lynn borough magistrate. Business and public life can have left little time for his own leisure yet he was an enthusiastic yachtsman and a member of the Royal Norfolk and Suffolk Yacht Club. In his later years he owned a steam yacht, the *Asteroid*, on which he made frequent cruises, narrowly escaping shipwreck during a gale off Blakeney around the turn of the century.

Alfred's last public act was to chair a meeting of the Lynn Charity Trustees in the Town Hall on Wednesday 2 December 1908. He died on Sunday 13 December. He was interred in the north-west portion of the churchyard at Titchwell amidst other members of the Dodman family.

Chapter 20

Agricultural shows

Norfolk Agricultural Association

Until 1862 the Norfolk Agricultural Association held an annual one day exhibition which alternated between Swaffham and Norwich. Then they decided to stage it at towns throughout the county and were rewarded with a steady growth in attendance. Takings on the gate at Dereham that year were £240, more than double the previous best. They were up yet again at Yarmouth the following year and reached over £500 at Lynn in 1864. Norwich hosted the first two day show in 1865 and, although there was not one in 1866, the years following saw a succession of successful shows at Fakenham, Downham, Attleborough, Harleston and Dereham. The Prince of Wales was Patron and President when the exhibition returned to Lynn on Wednesday and Thursday 19 and 20 June 1872. His attendance with the Princess for the opening attracted record breaking crowds; on that day alone nearly £1000 was taken.

Preparations for the royal visit

The royal visit was a welcome boost to trade at Lynn as the town and its people dressed in their finest. Samuel Parker, better known for equipping ships with masts, blocks and pumps, offered flags and poles, from sixteen to sixty feet in length, for hire or sale. He also advertised masts with wire rigging suitable for gardens. In High street William Boyce, John Thorley, T.R. Girling, and Messrs J. Kerkham & Son were vying for attention with their displays of the new season's fashions: costumes, dresses, shawls, millinery, bonnets, hats and caps of every kind, gloves, parasols, fancy goods and novelties. Arthur Bywater offered a range of ladies and gentlemen's kid and calf gloves, in black, slate, brown, green, pink and primrose, priced from 1s 9d to 3s 9d.

The work of decorating the town began on the Monday but finishing touches were still being added early on the Wednesday morning. By nine o'clock all was ready. The main streets were festooned with bunting, banners, evergreens and flowers as merchants, tradesmen and shopkeepers tried to outdo each other's displays. J. Defries & Sons, the renowned illuminators and decorators of London and Paris, had been hired to decorate the public buildings. They had also created a triumphal arch at the East Gate - thirty feet high with a gateway twenty feet high by twenty feet wide, ornamented with trophies and shields, and hung with crimson cloth edged in gold. The royal guests would be greeted with 'Welcome' in gilt letters on blue escutcheons, surmounted with the Prince of Wales' plume in silver embroidery. Meanwhile at Gaywood, on the route into Lynn, Capt Bagge and farmer William Warnes had supervised the decorations, including construction near the Post Office of a triumphal arch with three openings, adorned with evergreens, flowers and flags.

Lynn showground

The showground was set up on twelve acres of pasture in and around the Public Walks, several acres of which was occupied by canvas covered sheds in order to accommodate the unprecedented number of entries. The dominant feature was the pavilion in the paddock to the north of St John's walk, by the railway station, where the Association dinner would be held. Benjamin Edgington, of London, had been contracted to erect this monster marquee, weighing in at over seven tons. It was the largest canvas structure which had ever been seen at Lynn: 166 feet long; 86 feet broad; supported by three stout masts forty feet high, each carrying flags on staffs rising twenty feet higher. The exterior was ringed with 28 flagstaffs carrying gay-coloured banners. The interior was lined with crimson and white striped bunting and topped by a crimson valence with a yellow fringe. National flags surrounded each of the three masts. The ground was covered with wooden flooring as an insurance against wet weather. Under trees at the far end of the field, Edgington had erected two personal tents for the Prince and Princess. Each was 25 feet by 16 feet, lined with striped cloth, carpeted with crimson, and furnished elegantly by James Green of High street. The ground between these tents and the pavilion was laid out with a lawn and shrubbery.

Exhibition of implements

Lynn's engineers were at the forefront in the exhibition of implements. Frederick Savage had the largest display, featuring three traction engines, which incorporated levers for disengaging either or both of the driving wheels without stopping the engine. His ten horse power engine had wrought iron wheels six feet in diameter and cost £450. He showed an extensive collection of other machinery, including eight of Wood's American reaping machines, priced at £31 10s and manufactured in New York, where they could be produced much more cheaply than in Great Britain! Alfred Dodman also showed his traction engines but his greatest draw was a novel steam powered freezing machine manufactured by Siddeley and Mackey which could produce four or five pounds of ice per hour. Robert Southgate Baker, whose Phoenix works were in Blackfriars road, showed an extensive range of implements, including Corbett's elevator attached to a winnowing and weighing machine. This prize winning contraption enabled one man to run the whole operation, from winnowing to bagging, simply by continuously weighing the bag and stopping the flow of grain from the hopper when it was full.

Horticultural Society side-show

The King's Lynn Royal Horticultural Society took advantage of the royal visit to hold its first show of the season. Their marquees and the refreshment tents of Fiddaman & Lowe were clustered in Grey Friar's Tower field, opposite the entrance to the Walks and the showground. They had offered prizes amounting to £120 and had attracted a good number of entries. Spectators were immediately impressed by the extensive display of roses as they entered the main show tent but many retired swiftly, overcome by the oppressive atmosphere due to poor ventilation. Alongside, cottagers exhibited in a smaller marquee. At intervals throughout the day, the Lynn Rifle Corps Band entertained their visitors.

The royal visit

Visitors began pouring into Lynn on the Tuesday. Over ten thousand arrived by rail on opening day and most stayed for the second, when they were joined by another five thousand rail travellers. Even greater numbers arrived by road, especially on the second day when admission prices were lowered and farmers for miles around sent their labourers by horse-drawn waggons. On both days the streets of Lynn were thronged from early morning until far into the night.

On opening day the town was a glowing mass of colour, bathed in a brilliant sunrise. Church bells rang out at intervals. A stream of carriages entered the Walks, queuing to pass through an elliptical arch under a motif of plough and sheaves into the showground. Those on foot jostled their way alongside. By noon the town and showground had filled to overflowing and excitement intensified in anticipation of the royal arrival.

The Mayor's party waited nervously at the East Gate in a fine landau drawn by a pair of iron greys with a postilion. Promptly at half past two the cortège appeared: three open carriages, each drawn by four horses with mounted postilions. The Prince and Princess of Wales, the Earl of Leicester and Lord Sondes were seated in the first, attended by the equerries, General Probyn and Colonel Kingscote. The Marquis and Marchioness of Hamilton and Lady Ann Coke followed in the second; and Lord Suffield and the Hon Mrs E. Coke in the third. The Mayor, John Dyker Thew, resplendent in his scarlet robe of office, welcomed the Prince to Lynn and offered to guide him through the town to the exhibition. Mounted borough police commanded by Supt Ware led the way, followed by the Mayor's carriage and the royal cortège, with mounted police bringing up the rear. The crowds grew denser as the procession neared the Walks. Everywhere the Prince and Princess were greeted joyfully, some cheering loudly and enthusiastically while others quietly and politely raised hats and waved handkerchiefs. As they approached the entrance to the Walks and the showground, Lynn Rifle Corps Band greeted them with the strains of 'God Bless the Prince of Wales'.

The visit went smoothly until the Association dinner that evening. Soon after five o'clock the royal party and principal guests took their seats at tables on a raised, crimson-carpeted dais which ran the length of Edgington's pavilion. The town's treasures were proudly displayed. Behind the Prince were the ancient civic sword and silver maces while the celebrated King John's cup took pride of place on the table before him. Nearly a thousand guests, each of whom had paid 15s for the privilege, sat at twenty eight tables placed at right angles to the dais in two parallel rows. The first calamity came as Samuel Marshall of the Globe hotel, who had been entrusted with the catering, fought a losing battle with the close weather and was unable to present many of his choicest dishes. Guests were consoled by fine wines and the music of the band of the 7th Dragoon Guards, who were standing on the grass outside, drenched by frequent showers. The rain was so heavy that the pavilion's canvas roof became saturated and began to leak. Due to an unfortunate feature of the pavilion's construction, the table on the dais was most exposed to the drippings. The principal guests had to be sheltered under umbrellas but, fortunately, they were amused rather than annoyed by the inconvenience.

East of England Great Horse Show

When the East of England Horse Show came to Lynn in July 1876, under the patronage of the Prince of Wales, James Fiddaman proved himself to be 'indefatigable in his exertions for the public refreshment'. He also presented two cups, each valued at £8. The first was for horses not exceeding 15 hands, trotting in harness, 'action and speed considered, sulkies not allowed'; the second was for agricultural or cart stallions. The sixth annual show was held at Downham on Wednesday 31 July and Thursday 1 August 1878. There were prizes for cobs, trotting stallions, hunters, hackneys and roadsters. There was show jumping both days; and on the second day over seventy horses were entered for sale by Messrs Cruso and Hawkins. Crowds flocked to the ground. The event marked the end of an era for James, who announced that he would be giving up outdoor catering after twenty six years in the business. For the last time, his marquee was on the showground supplying refreshments and offering luncheon for gentlemen at 3s and for ladies at 2s 6d. At the showground, a week after the show, Messrs Cruso and Hawkins auctioned all James Fiddaman's catering paraphernalia, from cutlery to cheese trays, and hot water dishes to lamps. It was not the end of James' involvement in outdoor catering for he often returned to superintend the catering and to supply the wines and spirits, as he did at the Fakenham Show of the Norfolk Agricultural Association in 1883. On that occasion the refreshments were provided by Charles Skipper, the young baker, confectioner and pastry cook, whose shop was a few doors away from Fiddaman's hotel at number 2 Norfolk street.

Chapter 21

Wine and spirit merchants

Medicinal and cheering effects

When James took on the Wheatsheaf in 1852, there were about twenty wine and spirit merchants in the town. Most combined the trade with other interests. William Seppings in New Conduit street, Thomas and William Bagge in King street and Eyre & Chester in Bridge street were all brewers. Three of the innkeepers in Norfolk street were also spirit merchants in close competition with James: Thomas Smith at the Eagle, Jemima Clark at the Green Dragon, and Matthew Feaks, James' friend, at the Vine tavern. Several grocers were in the trade and serious competition came from James Burlingham, at 14 Norfolk street, on the corner with Broad street.

By 1858 James had built a good reputation for bitter ales and the best wines. He imported ginger brandy direct from the manufacturers and offered it at 2s 6d per bottle, bottle included. It was, he claimed, 'not to be surpassed in the world for its medicinal and cheering effects.' Throughout the 1860s and '70s prices remained remarkably steady. A dozen bottles of good port cost 18s and best quality Invalid's port 40s. Brandy was about 20s per gallon while a gallon of rum or gin could be as little as 10s 6d.

After 1860 wine consumption rocketed, principally amongst the middle classes whose purchasing power was increasing steadily. In 1859 Great Britain had imported nearly 700,000 gallons of wine from France and almost 5,000,000 gallons from Spain and Portugal; by 1876 imports from France had risen tenfold and from Spain and Portugal twofold. The trade became exceedingly profitable. Both James Burlingham and his successor, Robert Blackie, advertised regularly in the *Lynn Advertiser*. James Fiddaman relied on word of mouth and the publicity from his catering business and sporting interests. He made an exception in 1872, when he associated with Marchant & Co, London wine wholesalers, to offer Château Flotis in Lynn at 21s per case. He announced this plummy local wine of Toulouse, Côtes du Frontonnais, as a claret in direct competition with Robert Blackie's 1868 vintage claret at 18s per case. Based on the Negrette grape, it travelled well, was best drunk young and delighted his customers with its silky smoothness and flavours of liquorice and strawberry.

Robert Blackie

The Rev John Blackie was a Scot, born at Kelso into a family of Dissenting Presbyterians. He came to England to be trained at the Wymondley Academy in Hertfordshire and was ordained to Bungay Independent church in 1826. He died at the age of 43 leaving his wife Martha, nee Dryden, to bring up six children under eleven years old. One of these children was Robert, who was born at Bungay in 1834.

In his teens, Robert moved to Lynn where he became apprenticed to James Burlingham, the grocer and wine and spirit merchant, whose shop was at 14 Norfolk street on the junction with Broad street and opposite the Star inn. In 1861 he took over his master's business. The following year he married Emma, the elder daughter of Elizabeth and John Goddard Wigg who ran a chemist's shop at 3 Saturday Market place. They had a daughter Jessie in 1862 and a son Dryden Wigg in 1875. The family lived over the shop and the business prospered, occasionally exploring new ventures, such as the sole agency for anti-corrosion paint in the 1870s. Robert's health broke down in 1882; family and friends looked on helplessly until his death in 1884 at his home in Portland street.

The vanishing cheese

Robert Blackie offered choice groceries to accompany his fine wines. His supplies came from far and wide; many were delivered by the railway. In 1872, he ordered 33 cheeses from Messrs Swale, Almond and Goodliffe of Leicester. The Great Eastern Railway delivered them safely to the goods platform at Lynn station on Thursday 16 May. Porters discovered that one was missing as they loaded them into the delivery van. They informed Lynn police and also the railway police, since the cheese was strictly the property of the railway company at the time of its disappearance.

Next Saturday afternoon Mr Andrews, the foreman, was checking the railway company's stables, directly opposite the goods platform. He saw the missing cheese wrapped in a handkerchief under the straw beneath the manger. It was in good condition, except that a wedge had been cut from it. Andrews left it hidden and informed the police. Supt Ware posted PC Smith in plain clothes to keep watch on the stables from a nearby truck. It was gloomy and raining heavily as William Spalding and George Watts returned with their delivery vans. Smith saw them unharness their horses and bed them down for the night before they left for home, huddled against the driving rain. He checked the stables and found that the cheese had gone. Either Spalding or Watts must have concealed it under their clothes when they had left. PC Smith advised Supt Ware that the cheese had disappeared for a second time. They went to Exton's road where they arrested Spalding after finding most of the missing cheese in his pantry. Next stop was Albion terrace, Gaywood, where they saw Watts' wife hurriedly hide a piece of cheese in her pocket. They seized the cheese and took Watts into custody. The two portions corresponded exactly and the cheese was confirmed as the one which had vanished.

At Lynn Petty Sessions, Spalding and Watts pleaded guilty to stealing the cheese and were each sentenced to four months' imprisonment with hard labour.

Blackie's shop at 14 Norfolk Street
Advertisement reproduced from *Lynn Advertiser*

A runaway

James delivered via carrier to his customers in the surrounding towns and villages but used his own cart for deliveries in the town. In June 1876 the *Lynn Advertiser* recorded an incident as preparations were made for a delivery:

> On Saturday afternoon a grey mare belonging to Mr J. Fiddaman was being harnessed to a cart in the yard of the Wheatsheaf hotel and just as it was placed between the shafts it bolted into Norfolk street and made towards High street. In Norfolk street the animal capered to such an extent that it fell over but instantly gathering itself up it pursued its course along High street. There was a good deal of traffic in the street at the time and two or three horses which were being driven out of the town became frightened but were pulled up without doing any damage. The cart of Mrs Ewes, greengrocer, St Anne's street, was being pushed along High street by a boy when it was met by Mr Fiddaman's horse and knocked over, the contents of the cart being scattered in a somewhat promiscuous manner on the pavement. The boy was also knocked down but received no material injury. The horse continued its career to the Saturday Market place where it was stopped.

Quality, strength and cheapness combined

By 1880 James was also one of the largest bottlers of ale and stout in the county. He had begun using the new patent stoppered bottles which eliminated not only the need for a corkscrew but also the hazard from corks propelled by the products of secondary fermentation. He charged a refundable deposit of 1s 6d per dozen for corked bottles and 2s 6d per dozen for those with patent stoppers. He offered ales brewed by Bass, Younger and Guinness at prices between 3s 5d and 4s 6d per dozen Imperial pints. He bought stout from Guinness in hogsheads (52 gallons) for 57s and charged his cash customers 28s 6d for a kilderkin (18 gallons) or 3s 6d for a dozen Imperial pints.

The trade became increasingly cutthroat in the early 1880s as the Co-operative and other stores cut their prices to the bone. James responded by buying direct from the producers for cash, cutting out the partners, agents and travellers who ate into the profits, and offering his customers 'the full advantage of quality, strength and cheapness combined'. Blended Highland scotch, stouts, mineral waters and cigars were all made to his personal specification and sold under his own label at especially low prices. His advertisements in the *Lynn Advertiser* became more frequent as he listed wide selections of wines, brandies, whiskeys, liqueurs and cigars to suit every taste and pocket. In his wine vault Quarless Harris 1847 port at 138s per dozen lay nearby finest Tarragaso at 18s; Veuve Clicquot and Louis Roederer champagnes at 80s per case were stored alongside sparkling Saumur at only 26s. James delivered accounts quarterly but offered five per cent discount for cash. He published a trade list for caterers and offered them discounts for bulk purchases.

Half a dozen of James' earliest competitors survived into the 1880s. The Bagge and Eyre families remained prominent with Elijah Eyre & Co entering the retail trade in December 1883 with the opening of their wine, spirit, ale, stout and mineral water stores in the High street under the management of Robert L. Carpenter. Edmund Green succeeded his father on the Tuesday Market place. George Laws' business at 8 High street became Laws & Co. Competition was still keen in Norfolk street, where Matthew William Creak had set up as a grocer and wine and spirit merchant at number 33 by Paradise lane.

Chapter 22

Summer parties

A pleasant sea trip

In September 1878 James Fiddaman invited about 180 of his men friends for a day's fishing in Lynn Roads. He had engaged the steamer *Spindrift* after a chance discussion earlier in the year when her captain, John Hillman Howard, had been ferrying spectators from Common Staith quay to the Cut bridge for the King's Lynn Royal Aquatic Sports. The fare on that occasion had been 3d each but the scheme had not proved very remunerative.

The guests boarded *Spindrift* at nine o'clock on the morning of Wednesday 11th. *The Lynn Advertiser* reported:

> The weather was delightful, the sun shining brilliantly in a cloudless sky, the air fresh and balmy, and the water so calm that the most sensitive were not even reminded of the discomfort often attending the ups and downs of a marine voyage. It 'goes without saying' that the most hospitable preparations had been made to satisfy the cravings of a sea-appetite, and that the varied forms of thirst and connoisseurship in fluids were amply forestalled and gratified - the supplies including such 'teetotal' beverages as lime juice, soda water and lemonade, the happy medium of 'a drop of good beer', various kinds of wines and spirits, and cunningly concocted 'cups' of claret and champagne. The steamer, gaily decorated with flags from stem to stern, left the dock head soon after nine o'clock; and it was presently agreed that the proposal of putting out a net should be abandoned, on account of its inconvenience. In lieu of this, the trip was agreeably extended to the Lynn Well light ship, and an hour or so was devoted to inspecting that vessel and its appointments, and regaling its crew with a continuation of the songs, choruses and recitations which had beguiled the morning, in alternation with capital performances by the Lynn Volunteer Rifle Band,

under the direction of Bandmaster W. Green. Several of Mr Fiddaman's guests, being expert swimmers, indulged in 'headers' from the paddle-boxes, and gave a display of their natatory accomplishments with 20 fathoms of green water beneath them. During the afternoon, at a convenient stage of the return voyage, Mr J. Bray proposed from a commanding situation on the bridge, the health of their host ....

The toast was repeated several times and James' acknowledgement 'brought down the house' as he assured everyone that he had arranged the trip purely for pleasure and 'without the eye to business'! Capt Howard returned the *Spindrift* and her cargo safely to the dock head shortly after five o'clock.

This stag event was repeated but was not enjoyed by everyone unless it was an exceptionally calm day. Also, the ladies could not be invited and as James said at the time 'What was a party without them? It was like a ship without ballast'.

Enjoyable outing to Lenwade

In 1882 the fledgling Lynn and Fakenham Railway Company was extending its network with great enthusiasm. Its directors expected to open the line from Lynn to Norwich by the end of the summer, providing a much quicker service than the Great Eastern Railway. They also had plans to build a branch from Melton Constable via North Walsham to Yarmouth and were forging ahead with another line via Holt to Sheringham. They had invested large sums of money in these ventures and had spent much time getting approval from Parliament but traffic had built steadily and that year they had been able to declare a modest dividend.

James negotiated a good deal for a special train which would run from Lynn to Lenwade, ten miles short of Norwich and the furthest point of the line open to the public. About three hundred of James' and Jemima's friends accepted the invitation to join them for an outing on Wednesday 26 July. That day a train of fifteen saloon and first class carriages waited in Lynn station, headed by a new and powerful engine which had just been delivered to the Lynn and Fakenham Railway Company by Messrs Berger, Peacock & Co of Manchester. The guests began arriving at about ten o'clock and settled themselves into the carriages to read the morning's newspapers which had been so thoughtfully provided.

It was not long before the train steamed out of Lynn for a leisurely run to Melton Constable, stopping at stations en route to pick up more guests. They waited for about an hour and a half at Whitwell gazing upon the beauties of the surrounding scenery before being joined by the Carrow Works band who had travelled from Norwich on the Great Eastern Company's new line to Reepham. At two o'clock the party arrived at Lenwade, where James and Jemima had arranged for a lavish luncheon inside a large marquee in the station yard. The guests sat down, at tables decorated with ferns, flowers and foliage plants, to enjoy: boar's head, lamb, veal, roast beef, roast mutton, chickens, ducks, pigeon pies, tongues, ham and lobsters; followed by fruit tarts, French pastry, jellies, creams, iced raspberry and vanilla; and for dessert hothouse grapes, pineapple, greengages, strawberries and gooseberries. The wines and spirits flowed freely: champagne, sparkling hock, moselle, burgundy, claret, sherry, port and liqueurs. For the ladies there were cooling champagne and claret 'cups'; and for those with weaker constitutions, there was lemonade, soda and seltzer waters.

The band played while James and Jemima circulated amongst their friends: John J. and Matilda Lowe, John and Eliza Abel, Alfred and Mary Dodman, Frederick and Susannah Savage, J.K. and Louisa Jarvis, James and Lizzie Wenn, Thomas William and Frances Blomfield, and so many more that it seemed they would never manage to talk to each of them. John Dyker Thew and James Bowker presided over the formalities, leading toasts to the health of 'The Queen' and 'The Prince and Princess of Wales', 'the Town and Trade of Lynn', 'the Ladies', 'the Press', and of course 'Mr and Mrs Fiddaman', which last was drunk with musical honours and 'three times three'. It was left to Henry Dugmore of Bagthorpe hall to propose success to the Lynn and Fakenham Railway Company and to thank George Robinson Curson, its superintendent, who was in charge of the day's excursion. Every word was recorded by George Webster and William Sparkes, the newspaper reporters, who had been invited with their wives, to enjoy the party.

Many of the guests spent the afternoon strolling in the countryside, viewing Lord Canterbury's pretty old hall and park or visiting the village of

Witchingham, while others were content to listen to the band playing a selection of overtures, waltzes, polkas and quadrilles. The train set out for Lynn just after five o'clock, stopping to explore Fakenham and to enjoy more refreshments which were provided by John Lane of the King's Head. They reached Lynn at a quarter past nine that night having had a thoroughly enjoyable outing.

Invitation party at Holkham

James and Jemima chose Holkham for their party in 1883. They extended invitations to customers as well as friends and were accepted by nearly eight hundred people. On 18 July at ten o'clock, a special Great Eastern train pulled into Lynn station. Two saloon carriages, five first class, thirteen second and third class and two brake vans had been assembled behind a locomotive which was covered with flags, trophies, wreaths of flowers and foliage. Supt George Ware, accompanied by his wife Rebecca, was amongst the guests, reflecting on the good relationship which he and James had built since that unfortunate incident after the Regatta dinner. He was feeling particularly proud because the band of the Lynn borough police, which he had formed in 1881, had been engaged for the occasion and was playing in one of the carriages towards the middle of the train.

They reached Holkham at half past twelve, having stopped at every station along the way to pick up more guests. The sun shone brightly and most of the party dispersed to the beach. Meanwhile James and Jemima worked out how to cope with the serious damage which overnight gales had done to the large marquee in which luncheon was to have been served. They organised an overflow tent for the guests who would have to be displaced from the marquee and were ready to serve lunch at two o'clock. The Rev John Young, rector of Walsoken, who was looked upon as a sporting pastor because of his interest in yachting, said a grace before the guests relished the splendid meal. Henry Dugmore and John Dyker Thew presided over the usual toasts including one to the health of the Earl of Leicester for which John Overman returned thanks.

After lunch Edwin Mowll, of 4 London road Lynn, took photographs before the guests dispersed. Many went to Wells for the annual regatta, some returned to the beach, while others visited the palm house and gardens in

Holkham park or enjoyed the cricket match between Holkham and Rougham. Lord Leicester, who was watching the match with some friends, gave permission for the band to play, which they did for an hour or two.

Most guests returned to the marquee by half past six, in time to enjoy tea and other refreshments before boarding the train for Lynn at a quarter to eight. The train stopped for three quarters of an hour at Burnham so that James Fiddaman, accompanied by many friends and the band, could walk to the market place. Their visit had been expected because a crimson and white banner proclaiming 'Welcome' was strung across Front street between the house of Henry Howard, the carrier, and the draper's shop of Robert Hamilton. The band played for a quarter of an hour in front of the Hoste Arms, much to the delight of several hundred spectators. It was half past ten that night before the train reached Lynn and the last of the happy partygoers headed for home.

Chapter 23

Captain John Hillman Howard & the Spindrift

Family man

Capt John Hillman Howard was born at Deptford, Kent, in about 1828. He married Mary Bird at St Margaret's church Lynn on the 14th January 1849 and they went to live in Union lane. His mother-in-law, who was a nurse, moved in with them when baby John S. was born in 1852. Mary died and John married for a second time to Ann Maria Gardner, a mariner's widow with four children under the age of ten. They lived in Checker street for many years before moving to Ferry street, next door to the Crown and Mitre. They had three children: Mary A. in 1859, Eva in 1861 and William Walter in 1863. John was widowed again and by 1881 was living with his widowed mother, son William Walter Howard who was a cabinet maker, and his housekeeper, Mary Wilson, an unmarried twenty four year old with a five year old daughter Eliza. Capt Howard married for a third time at St Margaret's church on 12 August 1883 to Florence Regester Kitteridge, a seventeen year old from West Winch. They had four children: Ada, Archibald, Vivian and Florence. Capt Howard died in 1911.

Captain John Hillman Howard
Photograph courtesy of Nanette Rawlinson

Formation of the Lynn Steam Tug Company

Capt Howard was owner and operator of the steam tug *Judith*, which served Lynn harbour in the 1860s. Opening the Alexandra dock in 1869 attracted larger ships and heavier cargoes, which were beyond the *Judith*'s capability. Capt Howard decided to sell the *Judith* and form the Lynn Steam Tug Company (Limited) which would raise £2,000 to purchase a new tug. The Mayor, John Thorley, chaired a public meeting in the Town Hall on Saturday 5 March 1870 to discuss his proposals.

Capt Howard and J. Dixon presented the business case, showing that a return on capital of at least 20per cent should be achievable. Earnings in the past six months by vessels not belonging to Lynn had been £485: £285 towing thirteen vessels from Grimsby and Yarmouth to Lynn; and about £200 for ten vessels from the dock to the north. The tug *Judith*, operating to and from the Roads, had earned £250 in that time. They expected to take the lion's share of towage to and from Lynn and hoped for some of the traffic to the north from Wisbech and Boston. Operating costs were estimated at about £800 a year.

They had examined half a dozen of the best boats on the Tyne. The *Spindrift* was the most suitable for the Lynn trade and was within their means. She was a smart and powerful boat, built of wood by Dotchin at North Shields in 1869; 100 ft. long by 18 and three quarters ft. broad, drawing only 5 ft. of water when fully loaded. Her 50-horse power engines made her capable of 11 knots. The asking price was £1,950 but they might be able to get her for £50 less. Capt Howard reported that the vessel was well-built and seaworthy 'without finding anything to complain of except dirt, and that was a fault common to most of the Tyne boats, but one which was easy to remedy'. He had been most impressed to see *Spindrift* setting off to tow a 1,700 ton vessel round to the Tyne in conditions when 'scarcely another boat would venture, owing to the high seas'.

Share capital of £1,350 had already been promised by Messrs Cresswell, Jarvis, Burkitt, Holditch, Bond, Howard, Dixon, Howes, Coston, Fell and Charlton; Mr Brown, CE, added his name to the list. They took the Mayor's advice that they should proceed by mortgaging the boat to cover the balance of her price. A month later, Captains of vessels bound for Lynn, calling at Yarmouth or

Grimsby, could have the attendance of *Spindrift* within a few hours, by telegraphing to the Dock office King's Lynn.

Spindrift was in constant demand, business continued to grow and in 1879 the Company purchased the *Marie*, an iron vessel launched at Milton next Gravesend in 1876. Slightly smaller overall than *Spindrift,* she was fitted with three watertight bulkheads and certified to accommodate eight seamen.

Pleasure boat

Spindrift often took as many as 200 trippers to the cockle sands, Lynn roads or across the Wash. These voyages were enjoyable if there was a nice breeze but quite unpleasant if the wind was blowing strongly against the tide so that the sea was choppy. Bad weather frequently upset arrangements. On August bank holiday Monday in 1874 it had been announced that *Spindrift* would take day-trippers to Hunstanton and back at cheap fares. The morning was fine and by half-past nine about 200 had embarked. An exceptionally high tide had begun to ebb and there was a stiff breeze from the north-west. As the steamer entered the Wash, the sea was very choppy and trippers realised that they would experience some 'unpleasantness'. Capt Howard decided that it would not be safe to disembark at Hunstanton so instead he made a run for Skegness, where his passengers immediately went ashore, most grateful for terra firma. They returned to Lynn at ten that evening, having enjoyed the day despite the unexpected change of resort.

By the early 1880s, *Spindrift* was a major attraction at Skegness. Her most popular trip was across the Wash to Hunstanton at a cost of 3 shillings per head plus disembarking and toll charges on Hunstanton pier. If the tide was suitable, it was possible to leave the pier at half past eight in the morning and return about eight o'clock at night, having landed at Hunstanton soon after eleven and had time to visit the Prince of Wales' residence at Sandringham. The voyage routinely paused at Lynn Well lightship, six miles from Hunstanton and eleven from Skegness, where the crew worked a six week tour of duty and always welcomed a delivery of newspapers, fresh fruit and vegetables and the opportunity to post letters.

Sunk in the Nene

On Monday 5 August 1872, *Spindrift* had taken a party of trippers from Wisbech to Hunstanton during the day and had brought them safely back. That evening she was passing down the Nene on her way to Wisbech Eye in the Wash to pick up a tow, when she was caught in a violent storm. Capt Howard stopped the steamer just below the Foul Anchor, a mile or so above Sutton bridge. He swung her bows on to the ebb tide but one of her paddles caught some brushwood near the bank, her bottom was staved in, and her stern went under water. She quickly filled with water and her boiler fires went out. Capt Howard and his crew reached the bank safely. *Spindrift* slipped further into the river on the following tide and lay broadside to the East bank. She could not be recovered until noon on the following Friday, when she was taken up river to Wisbech for repair. Uninsured, the loss was carried by the shareholders of the Lynn Steam Tug Company, who had been earning good dividends up to that time.

Fire at Lynn

On the morning of Thursday 9 March 1876 *Spindrift* had got up steam in order to tow the Italian barque *Georgina* from the dock to sea en route for Philadelphia. Departure was delayed because one of the *Georgina*'s crew had deserted after stealing a gold watch belonging to a shipmate. *Spindrift*'s fires were banked up ready to tow out the *Georgina* next morning. All was well when the crew left her, lying at anchor in midstream opposite St Margaret's lane. At about eight o'clock, PC Taylor and two bystanders on the Marine Parade saw smoke coming from her cabin. They summoned the fire brigade. By half past eight the bells of St Margaret's church were ringing out, warning the town of fire, and a great crowd of spectators had gathered. Supt Ware and Sgt Barker were the first to get on board, attempting to extinguish the fire with buckets of water. Their efforts proved futile. Flames continued to spread with great rapidity and soon the whole of the after portion of the vessel was ablaze. The fire brigade put a pumping engine on a boat but the jet of water propelled them away from the fire. In desperation, they hauled *Spindrift* closer to the shore and smashed holes in her hull using axes and poles. She slowly sank. By high water only her mast and funnel were visible. *Spindrift*'s wooden hull was almost entirely destroyed: her stern by fire and other parts by the attempts to scuttle her. Her engines and boilers were not too badly damaged. She was valued at £3,400. Once again the loss fell on shareholders.

Bar Flat lightship

In 1878 the Town Council purchased a lightship for the Lynn channel in the hope that it would improve the port's safety and trade. The vessel, built of iron by Schlesinger and Co of Hull, arrived at Lynn dock in early August where she attracted large crowds of sightseers. At nine-o'clock on Thursday 12 September a select party assembled on board the *Spindrift*, which had been chartered to tow the vessel into position. Mr W. Burkitt, the chairman of the Port and Harbour Committee of the Town Council, was the host for the day and his guests included: the Mayor, W. Thompson; Sir Lewis Jarvis, chairman of King's Lynn Dock Company; John Dyker Thew; J.K. Jarvis, James Bowker and J. Paul, all members of the Port and Harbour Committee; Alfred Dodman; A.G. Russell, dock manager; F.J. Swatman, dock master; Mr Beaumont of the Hamburg Steamship Co; Charles Wise, manager of the East Coast Steamship Co; J.B. Rix representing the Carron Co; C.W. Harding, borough treasurer; and F.B. Archer, deputy Town Clerk.

On the lightship were Capt William Sparkes, a Trinity pilot, his mate Francis Shaul, and crewmen Hubbard Smith, William Little and Robert Powell. Mr Allison, whose firm had supplied the lighting apparatus, was to stay on board for the first week, instructing the crew in the working of the lamps. They fired their gun as *Spindrift* took them in tow, past vessels decked with bunting in the dock, and down the river to cheers from well-wishers on the shore. The sky was clear and the sun was shining. They were escorted for some of the way by Frank Cresswell's *Wild Duck*, Major Hare's yacht, and some others.

As they neared the mooring position by the entrance of the Lynn and Wisbech channels, a strong breeze blew up and there was occasional heavy rain. Poor visibility made it impossible to fix their position with great accuracy. In torrential rain, around eleven o'clock, the lightship's anchors were let go to ringing cheers. Her position would be adjusted when visibility improved. *Spindrift* came alongside while Mr Burkitt exhorted the crew to keep the vessel in good order and to be always at their posts. He presented two large and handsome Bibles, one for each cabin, and some other books which he hoped would help to relieve the boredom of their task. He promised that they would soon receive copies of the rules and regulations, which were still at the printers. A special supply of refreshments was put on board to celebrate the occasion and *Spindrift* headed for home. The weather cleared and the afternoon was most pleasant. They came up into the wind, tables were placed on deck, and Mr Burkitt entertained his guests to a splendid luncheon washed down by champagne and wines. A few appetites were upset by the pitching of the boat.

The voyage home was accompanied by alarms and excursions as *Spindrift* chased after two vessels which seemed to be going aground. Neither the *Peru* of Yarmouth, Nova Scotia, bound for Lynn with 6,000 quarters of maize for Messrs Burkitt, nor the *Aimwell* of London, also bound for Lynn, were actually in serious difficulty. Had the perceptions of those on board *Spindrift* been heightened by their day's mission? Or was their judgement clouded by the day's celebrations? The party arrived back at Lynn soon after five o'clock.

The last voyage

At six in the morning on Friday 8 March 1889 *Spindrift* left Lynn bound for Boston, from where she had been engaged to tow two empty lighters to Grangemouth. The crew that day were: James Barnard, mate; Henry Parker, engineer; Frederick Edgeley and Ed Townsend, firemen. It was low water, foggy weather, and a light breeze blew from the north. *Spindrift* arrived at Boston by nine thirty and left for Grangemouth an hour later towing the sloops, *Violet* and *Wave*, both of Boston, each with a crew of three. About five o'clock a breeze blew up from the south-east. It blew with increasing force. At ten that night, the *Violet* sprang a leak and sank within half an hour. Her crew transferred to the *Wave*.

By eleven, the wind had shifted from southerly to the north-east and increased to a gale, with snow and hail squalls. Waves were ten feet high, the edges of their crests breaking into Spindrift and the foam blowing in streaks. In a sudden squall, *Wave*'s tow rope parted. For two hours, Capt Howard tried to pass his own tow rope to the *Wave*. He eventually succeeded but not before *Spindrift* had shipped some very heavy seas, carrying away the port paddle casing and flooding the engine room. The gale was still increasing. Crests of waves began to tumble, topple and roll over; spray affected visibility. Capt Howard put his ship before the wind to run south for the Humber. About half an hour later they were struck by a terrific squall which caused *Spindrift* to broach and carried away her wheel chains. Engines and pumps fought a losing battle, until four o'clock on the Saturday morning when boiler fires were extinguished by the rising water.

Entirely at the mercy of the wind and waves, Capt Howard had to abandon the *Wave* and the six men on board her. *Spindrift*'s hand pumps were kept operating but three hours later her situation was hopeless. There were now seven feet of water in the ship. She was lurching violently and in imminent danger of capsizing. Two steamers passed nearby but took no notice of their distress flares. At seven that morning, they abandoned ship. Their lifeboat, only eleven feet long, was tossed about on the billowing seas, kept afloat by skilful seamanship and continuous bailing. After three hours, drenched to the skin, numbed with the cold and exhausted, they were rescued by the *s.s. Rocklands*, bound for Gibraltar. They were transferred to a Pilot Cutter off the Humber and then to the *s.s. Sea Gull*, landing at Grimsby at 3.15 in the afternoon and arriving back at Lynn at ten that night. The *Spindrift* had been seen to founder about a quarter to eleven that morning about twenty miles south-south-east from Flamborough Head. The six men on the *Wave* had been rescued by the smack *Research* and were landed at Grimsby on Sunday.

The steam tug Spindrift
Photograph courtesy of Nanette Rawlinson

Chapter 24

Never quite a gentleman

Silver salver

James was compassionate and generous, always ready to help the poor and needy or those in trouble and distress. In later years, when his business prospered, he could be relied on to support a worthy cause. In August 1878 he loaned his field on the Gaywood road for the Baptist schoolchildren's treat. When the foundation stone of St Margaret's church Highgate was laid by Miss Margaret Bagge on Saturday 30 August 1879, he was amongst the subscribers. He contributed to John Dyker Thew's Christmas appeal in 1881 which thanked the sixty or so engine drivers, stokers and guards of trains serving Lynn.

He donated 30 guineas to the West Norfolk and Lynn Hospital and became a life governor, able to recommend one in-patient and two outpatients for treatment each year. The hospital could accommodate about sixty inpatients and provided relief for 'the sick and lame poor'. The Prince of Wales was its patron; its vice-presidents included the Mayor of Lynn and many of the neighbouring nobility and gentry. Frank Cresswell was its treasurer for many years.

In autumn 1883 his closest friends decided to recognise his generosity and formed a testimonial committee: John J. Lowe; John Overman; James Bowker, who was the Mayor elect at that time; Joseph Prince; John Dyker Thew; William Pattrick, the Mayor; Charles Theophilus Ives, agent for the Atlas Fire and Life Office in Portland street; Henry J. Dugmore of Bagthorpe Hall; James Bacon, an Attleborough auctioneer; William G. Sheringham, a Fakenham merchant; and Joseph Feast, a Walsoken farmer.

The committee persevered despite James discovering what was planned and disapproving. With the exception of John Dyker Thew, who was ill and represented by his son Frank, they gathered for the presentation in a private room in Fiddaman's hotel on 7 November. The last act of William Pattrick's mayoralty was to present James with a purse containing fifty five guineas, a morocco bound book containing the names of subscribers, and an elegant and massive silver salver, richly chased and inscribed. James began his thanks but became overwhelmed by the occasion. James Bacon stepped in to explain what James had decided to do with the fifty five guineas. Jemima was to become a life governor of the Lynn hospital. Twenty guineas were to be given to the Hunstanton Convalescent Home, opened by the Prince of Wales in 1879 and built by public subscription as a thanksgiving for the Prince's recovery from serious illness. The remaining five guineas were going to the Norfolk and Norwich Hospital. When James had recovered his composure, he added that he wished to give, from his own pocket, a further thirty guineas to the Hunstanton Convalescent Home, ten guineas to the Royal Agricultural Benevolent Society and five guineas to the Eastern Counties Asylum for idiots at Colchester. His generosity was loudly applauded before the party adjourned to the dining room for an elegant luncheon and congratulatory toasting.

Into the finishing straight

A week or so later, James was laid low by cirrhosis, a condition from which he had suffered on and off for several years. He sought treatment from Dr Lowe who called in Sir James Paget and Sir William Gull, MD, FRCP, FRS. The latter was renowned as Queen Victoria's physician, prone to prescribe arsenic for rheumatic conditions and destined to be suspected of being 'Jack the Ripper' or, at the very least, someone who knew the murderer's identity!

Dr Lowe prescribed regular exercise and the medicine of hope. Each day James strolled around town, pausing with friends to reminisce about life at Lynn. He was constantly reminded of the excitement and hard work of the 1850s and early '60s when he and Jemima had established Fiddaman's hotel. Those were the years when the port of Lynn had steadily lost traffic to the railways and Lewis Whincop Jarvis, wealthy banker and solicitor, alderman and Mayor, had been its saviour. He had been the driving force behind the King's Lynn Dock Company which had constructed the Alexandra dock. In January 1878 he had been rewarded with a knighthood for his services to the town.

James approached John D. Ward, his solicitor, to put his affairs in order and asked his good friends Charles Ives and Arthur Dow, manager of King's Lynn gas company, to be the executors and trustees of his will. Jemima and her welfare were uppermost in his mind as he gathered his thoughts. He reckoned that his estate must be worth at least £8,000, a considerable fortune by any standards but one which gave him particular satisfaction because he had begun life without the advantages of inherited wealth or family connections. Jemima would want for nothing in her last years. She should have a substantial lump sum, the house in Wood street, which he had bought from John Parfrement, and an annuity.

He would soon be forgotten by his well-heeled clients, whose confidence and respect he had earned as wine and spirit merchant, public caterer or stake holder. He would be remembered for a while by his wide circle of middle class friends; Fiddaman's hotel would be his most lasting monument. If only his son had survived the storm in the Bay of Biscay, everything would have been so different. Frederick would have inherited the business and guided it through the difficult years which must lie ahead. Instead the trustees would have to realise most of his assets and it would be his nephews and nieces who would share the residue of his estate. He was blessed to have been a godfather five times over and each of his godsons had been a source of great pride and pleasure. Joseph Prince and Wessey Goodwin always sparked vivid memories of those times, twenty years ago, when he and their fathers had been so deeply involved in Lynn Races. Bertie Murrell had been born in 1878, a long awaited son and heir, after five daughters, for his good friend and neighbour William Murrell, the hairdresser, perfumer and tobacconist. Charles Fiddaman Boon had been born the same year, one of the ten children of his old friend William Boon, who farmed 1,000 acres at Tottenhill. Thomas Fiddaman Blomfield, the grandson of his lifelong friend John J. Lowe, was just a baby. He hoped that they would all remember him affectionately.

Happy memories flooded back as he chose items of his jewellery for his dearest friends. The gold rings, tie pins and scarf rings, most set with diamonds, pearls or rubies, were symbols of his wealth and his love of the turf; they had been the hallmarks of his style as a successful public caterer. James Bowker, William Pattrick and Supt George Ware would cherish such keepsakes, as would his friends in the service of the Prince of Wales: Charles Jackson and Charles Penny, gamekeeper and gardener at Sandringham; and Joseph Prince. Others would appreciate more practical consideration. James and Lizzie Wenn were having great success with their licensed luncheon rooms and restaurant in his property in the High street. Rather than selling the building, he would offer them the chance of renewing their lease for a further ten years at £60 per year. The rent would enable him to reward Elizabeth Hollingsworth, his most loyal barmaid, with an annual income of £25 while the remainder would go to his beloved Jemima.

James signed his will on Friday 4 January 1884 and enjoyed the weekend, satisfied that his affairs were in order. During the following week, he felt too poorly to take his daily exercise. He sat at home receiving visits from friends and agonising over the provisions in his will. By the weekend he was in a sombre mood, worsened by memories of baby Ann Elizabeth born exactly thirty years ago and taken from them so swiftly. On Saturday 19 January he added a codicil to his will making several minor bequests, increasing the provision for Jemima and giving his godson Joseph Prince a share of his estate's residue. He went to bed at midnight.

Fiddaman's field

James lay awake, wondering whether he might have played a greater role in public life. He had risen above his humble origins and lack of education. He had reached the stage when his business ventures did not require his undivided attention yet he had found himself fettered still by the malodorous reputation which lingered around his sporting transactions. Was the silver salver a sign of his rehabilitation?

Most of his friends were Conservatives and so was he, although he had never played a particularly active role in politics. He remembered the thrills of 1868, when the newly formed Lynn Loyal and Constitutional Association had won its first victory. In February he had served its annual dinner in the Music Hall at the Athenaeum, where Lewis Whincop Jarvis, the Association's president, had led nearly four hundred members in an enthusiastic welcome of Sir William Bagge and the Hon Thomas De Grey, the MPs for West Norfolk. November had brought a general election. Lord Stanley had triumphed yet again and the Hon Robert Bourke had beaten Sir Thomas Foxwell Burton, the Liberal, into third place. William Armes and George Holditch had lodged a petition against Bourke's election alleging bribery, 'treating' and intimidation by more than a dozen prominent members of the Association, amongst them Lewis Whincop Jarvis and Frederick Savage. Their case had centred on the meetings which J.K. Jarvis, Bourke's election agent, had organised at the numerous public houses owned or supplied by Conservative brewers, including James Bowker of Eyre & Co and Richard Bagge. These occasions had supposedly provided John Dyker Thew and others with opportunities to curry favour by offering bribes or treating voters to drinks and meals. The petition had been tried at Lynn County Court in March 1869 and been dismissed. He and John J. Lowe had served a grand banquet as the Association had celebrated!

Over a thousand people had packed into the Corn Exchange, surrounded by flags and banners proclaiming 'Stanley for ever' and 'Bourke for ever'. The place had been brilliantly illuminated by gaslight; a royal crown, fashioned with gas jets, had hung behind the head table. He and John J. had hired seventy waiters for the occasion, not all of them reliable. Sweet memories turned to sour as he remembered how he had tried to discipline one of them, Henry Nichols, for not pulling his weight. He had been so exasperated that he had ended a verbal exchange with a blow to the man's head. The magistrates had taken a dim view of his behaviour and had fined him 5s with 15s costs.

James drifted into a fitful sleep. He dreamt of Lynn Races, crowds shouting encouragement from the grandstand, and his horses galloping to the finish. He awoke to memories of the 'Great Lynn Borough Steeplechase Day', not a horse race but nonetheless a race and one which amused him greatly. Frank Lockwood, one of the Liberal candidates in the 1880 Lynn borough election, had invented the occasion to enliven his address at the Music Hall. He had ended the evening with the story of his dream in which Sir W. Ffolkes, the Hon Robert Bourke, Lord Claud Hamilton and himself were all runners on 'Fiddaman's field'. The audience had roared with laughter as John Dyker Thew was portrayed as the proprietor of a political popgun, running about the field and selling correct cards at 2d each, while 'very fierce about the face and very mild about the legs'. Sir Lewis Whincop Jarvis had fared little better 'with a yellow hat on, surrounded by his large and intellectual family in yellow pinafores'. Yet no one had laughed at Fiddaman's field.

His old servant Martha Cozens was sitting by him, holding his ice cold hands, listening to his shallow and irregular wheezing, when he died at twenty minutes to 11 on the Sunday night. The best attentions of Dr Lowe, Sir James Paget and Sir William Gull had only postponed the inevitable. Next day flags were at half-mast, blinds drawn and windows partially shaded throughout Lynn as people mourned the passing of their popular townsman, a wealthy tradesman but perhaps never quite a gentleman.

Washington funeral car

At noon on the following Thursday, Samuel Marshall's Washington funeral car left Fiddaman's hotel carrying James in a richly-polished oak coffin. Jemima, family and close friends followed in twelve mourning coaches. They passed down Norfolk street, Railway road and London road on their way to the cemetery in Hardwick road. Hundreds more friends, four abreast, joined them at the entrance to the Public Walks. Each of James' employees had been provided with a good suit of mourning, including a hat or bonnet and a pair of boots. Amongst them were his cellar man James Cozens, barmaids Elizabeth and Rose Hollingsworth, and clerk Frederick Whin Dawson.

Rev Dale, the vicar of St Margaret's, laid James to rest in a brick vault on the west side of the mortuary chapel. In the town's almshouses that night sixty or so inmates remembered 'Fiddy' with affection, dreaming how they would spend the 20s that he had left each of them.

Chapter 25

Legacy

Jemima sold the business to Nicholls, who tried to build on Fiddaman's reputation as a wine and spirit merchant. The sale included cases, casks, jars and bottles, both on the premises and out in the trade, but the public failed to return them. By June 1884 Nicholls had run out of bottles and had to place an urgent appeal in the *Lynn Advertiser* asking customers to return their empties at once. Fiddaman's hotel had passed into the hands of Nicholls & Campbell Ltd when around 1911, as a lad of fifteen, Collins Webber Langwade began work there as a billiard marker. Two years later he was called up to serve in the Middlesex Regiment. He returned to the hotel in 1918 to take charge of the billiards saloon, becoming a highly proficient player who played many exhibition matches. He managed the hotel from 1942 until his retirement in 1953. In the winter of 1966/7, Fiddaman's hotel was closed; the building was demolished soon afterwards to make way for redevelopment.

Jemima retired to London, where she lived at 42 Lessar avenue, just across the road from Clapham Common, with her old friend, Eliza Stainton Abel, the widow of John Abel whose horses had been so successful at Lynn Races. She died on 8 August 1907 and was laid to rest alongside James in Hardwick road cemetery. She had appointed Eliza Abel and Albert Berenburg as the executors of her will. She left £100 to her friend Theresa Forder and the house in Wood street Lynn to Fanny Blomfield, the mother of Thomas Fiddaman Blomfield. The bulk of her estate went to Eliza, her faithful companion. Albert Samuel Berenburg, the son of a German immigrant, was a paper merchant who lived near Dulwich in Surrey. Jemima left him the furniture and effects in her drawing room and an equal share with Eliza of the residue of her estate. She also left him the fine silver salver inscribed:

> Presented with 55 guineas, which he intends devoting to charitable purposes, to Mr. Jas. Fiddaman, by numerous friends, as a token of their high esteem for him and for his many acts of unbounded liberality and kindness. 1883.

We often wonder whether the salver has survived two World Wars and, if so, what people conjure up for the life which lies behind the inscription.

NEW VAUXHALL CONCERT HALL
LYNN.

GREAT ATTRACTION,
FOR
Two Nights Only,
Monday, Aug. 4th, Tuesday, 5th.

MR. J. FIDDAMAN

Begs to announce that he has engaged at a great expence the following celebrated artists

Mr. W. BRATTON,
From the Haymarket Theatre, London.

Mr. Harry POOLE,
The English Botesina also the renowned

Professor Trevori,
Who will appear in a grand vocal and instrumental

CONCERT,
Which will embrace the greatest novelties of the season.

Messrs. POOLE and BRATTON will perform a solo upon a single violin, which is pronounced to be the greatest wonder in the Musical World.

Mr. BRATTON will perform the following celebrated Solos the Carnival de Venice, Carnival de Cula, imitating singing Birds, Cuckoo Solo, also a Solo upon one string A LA PAGANINI.

Mr. HARRY POOLE will perform several Solos upon the Contre Bass, including All is Lost Now, La Somnambula, La Multi, and will go through a variety of astonishing performances too numerous to mention.

PROFESSOR TREVORI

Will still continue to delight all that hear, and in the course of the evening, will sing the

RATCATCHER'S DAUGHTER,
in character

Remember, this is Trevori's farewell of Lynn, as he appears in London on Monday next, a variety of entertainments will be produced Sentimental singing by eminent artists. Notwithstanding the great expence attending this engagement, in order to give every body a treat it will be

ADMISSION FREE
To commence at eight o'clock,

Remember positively for 2 nights only.

CADMAN, PRINTER, LYNN.

Photograph courtesy of King's Lynn Museums

Chronology of significant events

1800	East Gate Lynn demolished
1801	Act of Union of Great Britain and Ireland - Union Jack official flag
	Electric arc lamp invented by Sir Humphrey Davy
	Population of Lynn 10,096
1802	Market house erected in Saturday Market place at Lynn
1803	London Road Lynn - building begins
1807	First Ascot Gold Cup
1811	Population of Lynn 10,259
	Unitarian Church built in Norfolk Street Lynn
1815	Building of The Theatre near the Greyfriars tower at Lynn
1820	George IV succeeds George III
	Ladybridge brewery in Bridge street Lynn founded by Elijah Eyre
1821	New bridge over Eau Brink Cut opened at Lynn
	Eau Brink Cut opened by passage of 'Swiftsure' steam packet
1822	St. James' hospital at Lynn rebuilt
1824	Public meeting at Lynn Town Hall to launch a "Gas Light Company"
1826	Road/bridge built over Cross Keys Wash through Marshland to Lincs.
	Lynn cattle market opened at Paradise field
1827	William Aickman established his foundry at Lynn
1828	Establishment of effective police force in London
	New mill to supply water built at Kettlemills on Gaywood River Lynn
1830	William IV succeeds George IV
	Beer Act
	Lynn Market House constructed in Tuesday Market Place
1831	Population of Lynn 13,370
	Turnpike Act to amend roads branching from East and South gates
	Ouse Bank Commissioners awarded £46,000 to maintain river bank
	Cholera strikes Lynn
1832	Reform Act gives vote to upper middle classes

1834	National education begun
	Poor Law Amendment Act
	175 gas street lights in Lynn
1835	Municipal Corporations Act
	West Norfolk & Kings Lynn Hospital opened off London road Lynn
	St. James' Workhouse becomes the Union Workhouse
	122 vessels registered at Lynn Custom house
1836	Birth of Mrs Beeton
1837	Queen Victoria succeeds William IV
	Invention of telegraph by S F B Morse
	Sir William Bagge becomes MP for West Norfolk
1838	First steam crossing of the Atlantic
1839	First Grand National at Aintree
	First true bicycle constructed by Kirkpatrick Macmillan
1840	Victoria marries Prince Albert
	Penny post established in Great Britain
	Development of photography
1841	Robert Peel becomes Prime Minister
	Population of Lynn 16,039
1842	British school opened in Blackfriars Road Lynn
	Conversazione and Society of Arts formed at Lynn
	Establishment of the Lynn Advertiser & West Norfolk Herald
1844	First Norfolk railway opened between Norwich and Yarmouth
1846	Repeal of Corn Laws begins Free Trade
	Lynn to Downham & Narborough railway line opened
1847	Working day for women and children limited to 10 hours
	New Cut opened to drain Middle Level of Fens
	Railway from Lynn to Downham extended to Ely, thence London
1848	Lynn MP Lord Stanley visited town
	Lynn cattle market expanded on to site of old Framingham's hospital
1849	St Margaret's National School for 500 pupils in Greyfriars road
1850	235 gas street lights in Lynn
1851	Great Exhibition opened in Hyde Park
	First cable to Calais
	Population of Lynn 19,355
1852	William Lee's Report into Sewage, Drainage, etc. of Lynn

1853	Estuary Cut opened improving port of Lynn access to Wash
1854	Britain and France declare war on Russia - Crimean War
	Lynn's first public baths built on Common Staithe Quay
	Corn Exchange built at cost of £2,500 on site of Lynn Market House
	Athenaeum opened on Baxter's plain Lynn at a cost of £6,400
	The Stanley library founded at Lynn
	Tower of St. James' Chapel fell down
1855	Borough cemetery opened on Hardwick road Lynn
1856	End of Crimean War
	Formation of Lynn Gas & Coke Company (Limited)
	Boal quay built by the Corporation of Lynn near the Friars
	New King's Lynn Union Workhouse completed in Exton's road
1857	Sepoy mutiny in India
1858	Formation of Volunteers
	Drinking fountain and public lamp erected in Tuesday Market place
1859	Formation of 5th or Lynn Company of Rifle Volunteers
	Savings Bank built in St James Street Lynn
	Anglican St John's Church opened in Lynn
1860	Refreshment Houses & Wine Licences Bill
	Church of England Young Men's Society commenced at Lynn
1861	Death of Prince Consort
	Population of Lynn 16,701
	Lynn County Court built
1862	Prince of Wales acquired Sandringham Estate
	Creation of Great Eastern Railway
	Station built at South Lynn for Midlands & North
	Railway line from Lynn to Hunstanton opened
1863	Great Eastern Railway Co. offer part funding for dock
	1,780 tons of corn passed through port of Lynn
	1,100 tons each of wheat and barley sold at Lynn Corn Exchange
1864	Pilot Office erected on Common Staithe Quay
	First exhibition of Lynn Horticultural Society
1865	Transatlantic cable completed
	Lynn Dock & Railway Company set up to build Alexandra Dock
	High or Stone Bridge at Lynn taken down
1866	Purfleet at Lynn culverted

1868	Foundation stone laid for Alexandra dock at Lynn
1869	Opening of Suez Canal
	Lynn Alexandra Dock opens - used by 165 vessels
1870	Foster's Education Act (Compulsory)
	Electric incandescent lamp invented by T.A. Edison
1871	Prince of Wales (Edward VII) catches typhoid fever
1872	Central Lynn's wooden railway station replaced
	First board meeting of West Norfolk Farmers' Manure Co. Ltd.
1873	Invention of pianoforte by J. Broadwood
1874	Sir William Bagge retires as MP for West Norfolk
1876	Invention of the telephone by A.G. Bell
1877	Victoria proclaimed Empress of India
1879	Zulu War - massacre of British soldiers
1880	79 vessels registered at Lynn Custom house
	Over 580 vessels used the Alexandra dock Lynn
1881	Population of Lynn 17,362
	Formation of Kings Lynn Police Band
1883	Bentinck Dock Lynn opened
1884	General Gordon reaches Khartoum
	Stanley Library built at Lynn
	Jermyn & Perry's shop at Lynn burnt down
1885	General Gordon killed at Khartoum
	Frederick Savage patented device for galloping horses on carousel
1887	Queen Victoria's Jubilee

Mayors of Lynn

1837	John Platten		1864	William Monement
1838	Francis Hulton		1865	John Osborne Smetham
1839	John Platten		1866	" " "
1840	Edward Bagge		1867	Walter Moyse
1841	James Bowker		1868	John Thorley
1842	John Wayte		1869	" "
1843	" "		1870	Edwin Elmer Durrant
1844	Robert Pitcher		1871	John Dyker Thew
1845	Francis Cresswell		1872	John Osborne Smetham
1846	Thomas Augustus Carter		1873	" " "
1847	Edward Everard		1874	Edwin Elmer Durrant
1848	William Seppings		1875	George Holditch
1849	Walter Moyse		1876	John Dyker Thew
1850	" "		1877	William Thompson
1851	Richard Bagge		1878	Thomas Johnson Seppings
1852	Lionel Self		1879	" " " ob.
1853	John Platten		William Thompson	April 19, 1880
1854	John Marsters		1880	Thomas Martin Wilkin
1855	William Seppings		1881	John Osborne Smetham
1856	Robert Cook		1882	William Pattrick
1857	John Osborne Smetham		1883	James Bowker
1858	Walter Moyse		1884	" "
1859	Lionel Self		1885	John Dyker Thew
1860	Lewis Whincop Jarvis		1886	William Burkitt
1861	" " "		1887	George Smith Woodwark
1862	" " "		1888	George Gold Sadler
1863	William Burkitt		1889	Frederick Savage

The Mayor took office from the end of October or beginning of November; in 1949 it became May